Acc 4201   301

This book is to be returned on or the last date stamped below

ANDREW MARVELL
SCHOOL LIBRARY
PLEASE RETURN

ANDREW MARVELL
SCHOOL LIBRARY
PLEASE RETURN

EARTH CARE

People
& Society

Miles Litvinoff

Heinemann

Editor   *Designer*
Judy Garlick   Malcolm Smythe
Managing editor   *Art editor*
Lionel Bender   Ben White

PEOPLE AND SOCIETY (Earthcare)
was produced for Gaia Books by
Bender Richardson White, Uxbridge, UK.
This edition first published in Great Britain in 1996
by Heinemann Library
Halley Court, Jordan Hill, Oxford OX2 8EJ
a division of Reed Educational & Professional
Publishing Ltd
Oxford Florence Prague Madrid Athens
Melbourne Auckland Kuala Lumpur Singapore Tokyo
Ibadan Nairobi Kampala Johannesburg Gaborone
Portsmouth NH (USA) Chicago Mexico City São Paulo

Copyright © Gaia Books Limited, London 1996
Gaia Books Limited
66 Charlotte Street, London W1P 1LR and
20 High Street, Stroud GL5 1AS

All rights reserved including the right of reproduction in
whole or in part in any form.
Reproduction MRM Graphics, Winslow, Bucks, England
Printed in Spain
00 99 98 97 96
10 9 8 7 6 5 4 3 2 1
ISBN 0 431 07722 3

British Library Cataloguing in Publication Data
Litvinoff, Miles
People & Society. – (Earth Care)
1. Persons – Juvenile literature 2. Social sciences
– Juvenile literature
I. Title
301

Acknowledgements
Production: Kim Richardson, Susan Walby
Direction: Patrick Nugent, Pip Morgan, Joss Pearson;
Publisher Liason Hannah Wheeler, at Gaia Books.
Illustrations David Ashby; Norman Barber (Linden Artists); Martin Camm (Linden Artists); Jim Channel (Linden Artists); Stefan Chabluk; David Cook; Bill Donohoe; Eugene Fleury; Chris Forsey; Aziz Khan; David Mallot; Gary Marsh; Francesca Pelizzoli; John Potter; David Salariya; Ann Savage; John Shipperbottom; Rob Shone; Nicky Snell (Virgil Pomfret Agency); Clive Spong (Linden Artists); Roger Stewart (Virgil Pomfret Agency); Alan Suttie; George Thompson; Shirley Willis.
Photographs The publishers would like to thank the following for permission to reproduce photographs: pages 4–5 David Keith Jones/Images of Africa. 10 Julio Etchart/Oxfam. 14 Nancy Durrell-McKenna/Oxfam. 16 Howard Davies/Oxfam. 18–19 (main) Kay Willis/Oxfam; (rest) Mike Goldwater/Oxfam. 24–25 Kim Richardson/Alba Publishing. 26 Raqu/Oxfam. 31 US Geological Survey. 33 Environmental Picture Libary/Leslie Garland. 35 Environmental Picture Library/H. Girardet. 38–39 (main) Maryam Iqbal/Oxfam; (rest) Liz Clayton/Oxfam. 41 Mike Goldwater/Oxfam. 42 Dr J.F. Oates.
Cover photographs Image Bank, Robert Harding Picture Library
Cover design Simon Balley Design Associates

The publishers would like to thank Koos Neefjes, Amanda Barker, and Fred Martin for their helpful comments on the text. Bender Richardson White would like thank John Stidworthy for help in planning the book, and Liz Clayton and Anna Coryndon at Oxfam for producing the Gaiawatch articles and supllying photographs.

MILES LITVINOFF is a specialist writer and editor of books on environment, development, and human rights for children and adults. He works as an editor for the Minority Rights Group, a human-rights organization in London, and tutors the Open University environment course. He is author and editor of many successful titles, including *The Greening of Aid: Sustainable Livelihoods in Practice* (co-editor, 1988), *The Earthscan Action Handbook for People and Planet* (1990), *Ancestors: The Origins of the People and Countries of Europe* (co-author, 1992), the *Junior Cultural Atlas series* (1989–94), and *The World Minorities Directory* (1996).

CONTENTS

About this Book	3
HUMANKIND	4
Needs & Rights	6
World at Work	8
Clever or Wise?	10
People & Health	12
Out of Work	14
Rights in Crisis	16
Gaia Watch - The Macuxi of Brazil	18
Better Health	20
Sharing Skills	22
CIVILIZATION	24
Living in Cities	26
World Factory	28
Communication	30
Chaos in the City	32
Have & Have-nots	34
World at War	36
Gaia Watch – Community Groups in Pakistan	38
Action for Cities	40
Closing the Gap	42
Useful Contacts	44
Glossary	46
Index	48

ABOUT THIS BOOK

This book is part of a four-title series that explains our place on the Earth, the environmental problems we face, the kind of solutions we need, and how people are already working to put good ideas into practice.

Underlying the approach in the books is the Gaia theory, named after the Earth goddess of ancient Greece. The space scientist James Lovelock first proposed the Gaia theory in the 1970s. The theory suggests that the biosphere – the thin layer between the Earth's rocky surface and outer space, the home of plants and animals, including ourselves – is a living organism. Life has created and maintained the conditions it needs for its own survival. The Earth does not need the human species, but we may not survive unless we safeguard the natural resources on which we depend.

Another important idea is justice, or fairness. The brutal poverty experienced by one person in every four involves the denial of many basic interconnected human rights. Poverty on this scale is largely, although not only, the result of human choices and actions. Better decisions by individuals, small groups, larger communities, countries and governments can therefore make the world a fairer place.

Many of the most urgent environmental problems result from extremes of wealth and poverty. The very rich cause immense environmental damage by consuming too much, while the poor degrade their surroundings in the struggle to survive. Working to safeguard our environment and working for a fairer world are closely connected.

People and Society takes a human-focused look at global issues, firstly with an emphasis on the rights and needs of individual people, and the problems people face, and then by considering societies and the modern world more broadly. The first chapter, **Humankind,** explores our human potential, human needs and rights, and how these can best be fulfilled. After a discussion of such major problems as overpopulation, ill-health, and unemployment, the chapter suggests how we might ensure that all the world's people enjoy a reasonably good quality of life. The second chapter, **Civilization,** considers humanity as a whole. It describes both the benefits and the disadvantages arising from modern society, including poverty and the threat of war, before considering the action we can take to improve matters.

Each chapter contains information and ideas laid out in self-contained two-page sections, or "spreads". Each spread combines text, maps, diagrams, and photographs, and takes one of three viewpoints: Resources, Problems, or Solutions. Both chapters also include an illustrated "Gaia Watch" case study, provided by Oxfam, and two further features: "Do you know?" boxes provide additional facts, figures, and examples not contained in the main text, while "Home action" boxes suggest what we can do within our community to tackle problems.

At the end of the book, before the index, is a list of useful contacts in the United Kingdom – including government departments, industry bodies, and a host of voluntary and campaigning groups – and a glossary of terms. We explain new, difficult, and important terms the first time they are used in the text: these terms are in **bold** if they appear in the glossary. Some terms, however, need a brief mention here.

We often describe countries as either "developed" or "developing" (although the terms do not fit all countries equally well). Developed countries are those where large-scale industry, based on burning coal, oil, and gas, is well established and usually the main source of jobs and wealth creation. These countries control most international trade and are generally rich. Developing countries are those where farming is still the main way of life. Most developing countries are poor. There are many more developing than developed countries. We also use the terms "North" and "South', broadly to mean the same as "developed", or "rich", and "developing", or "poor". All industrialized countries, apart from Australia and New Zealand, are in the northern hemisphere; most developing countries are in the southern hemisphere.

We use the US dollar as the standard measure of money, which is common for international comparisons. As a rough guide, you can convert dollars to pounds sterling on the basis of $1.50 = £1.

Abbreviations
The following abbreviations are used in the series:

%: per cent	m^2: square metre	g: gram
cm: centimetre	ha: hectare	kg: kilogram
m: metre	m^3: cubic metre	t: tonne
km: kilometre	km^3: cubic kilometre	kW: kilowatt
		kWh: kilowatt-hour

HUMANKIND

"Local groups are now demanding a halt to the destructiveness of modern society. It is through such groups . . . that change will come about . . . not imposed from above but created from below by ordinary people."

EDITORS OF *THE ECOLOGIST*,
a leading UK environmental magazine

People are the greatest **resource** the Earth has – and its biggest problem. Clever, adaptable, skilful, and strong, we spend much of our time ignoring the needs of our fellow human beings, and our shared **environment**, and thinking of our own private wishes instead. We take advantage of each other's difficulties and sometimes act with cruelty and violence towards each other. It often seems as if we will never be able to control the increase in human numbers, or stop damaging our natural surroundings and harming others. But hope is at hand. We can and do learn from our mistakes, and this fact offers everybody a real opportunity to make the world a better place.

Zulu boys at work with oxen and plough in South Africa. In many traditional **communities**, learning to work the land is an important part of children's family upbringing.

INTRODUCTION

HUMANKIND

NEEDS & RIGHTS

If you are reading this book you are literate; you probably have a comfortable home and attend school or college; and you can look forward as an adult to a choice of occupation and a say in decisions that affect your life. Potentially, you are one of tomorrow's problem-solvers rather than a part of one of its problems.

DID YOU KNOW?

Richest doesn't always mean best
While richer, **developed countries** are usually in a stronger position than poorer, **developing countries** to meet their people's needs and respect their rights, some countries do far better or worse than we might expect. The USA, for example, which has the world's largest industrial **economy**, has 100,000 homeless and 500,000 badly fed children; while Cuba, a poor country, has achieved impressive standards – especially in **primary health care** and maternal and child health.

About 5700 million people live on Earth today. Between us, we surely have the knowledge and skills to make the world a fit place for all to live in; a world in which humankind is at peace with the rest of nature. For this to happen, every human being needs the chance to develop his or her full potential.

The world is full of active, able people, young and old, in every **country**, who are making positive contributions to society. But, sadly, millions of others cannot develop fully, because they are denied one or more of their needs and rights – the things you believe you are entitled to as a member of society.

Since the dawn of history some human beings have suffered hunger, poverty, slavery, cruelty, and death at the hands of others. Yet, it can be argued, some groups of people, such as the African San (Bushmen), have avoided war and developed fair ways of living together that harm nobody.

Putting the wrongs right

We have a broad range of tools with which to solve our problems: laws, which set rules for human behaviour; technology, which helps get jobs done; and democratic politics, with which we can make decisions together. A great belief in humanity's problem-solving abilities led the United Nations to proclaim the Universal Declaration of **Human Rights** in 1948, with the words "all members of the human family . . . are born free and equal in dignity and rights . . . and should act towards each other in a spirit of brotherhood."

Despite any progress we may have made in improving the way we treat our fellow human beings, more people across the globe suffer serious deprivation today than ever before. Only when the needs and rights of these people have been properly satisfied will we be able to meet with confidence the other challenges facing the world.

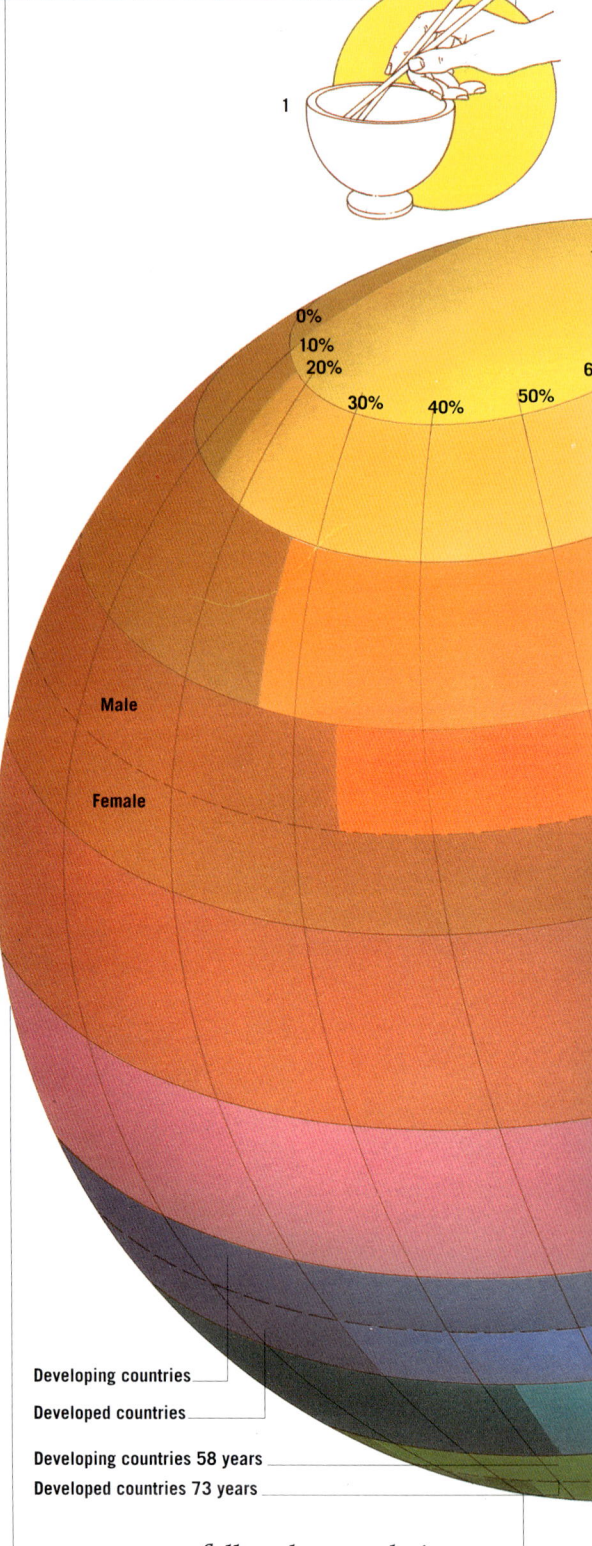

Developing countries
Developed countries

Developing countries 58 years
Developed countries 73 years

RESOURCES

1 Enough food to eat is essential for all living things. Yet 800 million people do not eat enough to stay healthy.

2 Infant death in the developing world is such that seven out of every 100 babies die before their first birthday, compared with one in 100 in developed countries.

3 Primary schooling is every child's right. More than 90 per cent of all children start school, but 40 per cent don't finish primary education.

4 Literacy has improved worldwide since the 1960s. Even so, half the world's females and a third of its males cannot read or write.

5 Adequate housing includes access to proper **sanitation** facilities. Only a quarter of humanity has these.

6 Government welfare helps people who cannot work or earn. Millions have no such protection.

7 Basic freedoms include being able to expresss your opinion and vote in elections. Many people lack these freedoms.

8 Work is another human right, a source of self-respect as well as income. More than a third of people of working age are unemployed or **underemployed**.

9 Life expectancy varies widely. People in some parts of the world die, on average, in their 40s; elsewhere they can expect to live 30 years longer.

Needs and rights in selected countries
Below are three examples of how different countries provide for the needs and rights of their citizens. The nine discs in each diagram match the numbered needs and rights in the main illustration (left).

China, a poor country with a population of 1221 million, has improved the lives of most of its people since 1950. The availability of food, education, employment, and life expectancy are all better than before. But many citizens, especially girls and orphans, suffer cruelly, and there is little **democracy** or freedom.

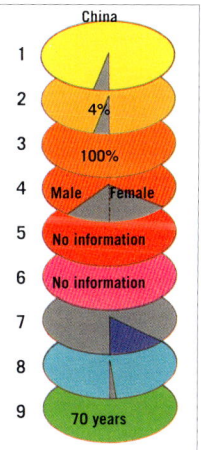

Costa Rica, in Central America, disbanded its army 40 years ago and has enjoyed peace and prosperity since, unlike its neighbours. All Costa Ricans attend primary school and most are **literate**. They have political freedom and good life expectancy. Welfare is limited, but unemployment is low. Costa Rica's environmental record is good.

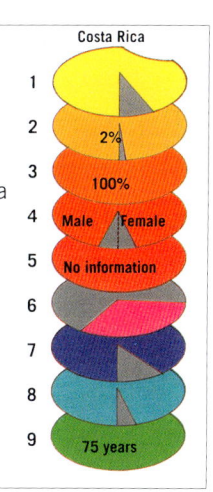

Denmark is highly successful at providing for its citizens. It has high literacy, low **infant mortality**, and high life expectancy. Some Danes are unemployed, or do not receive adequate welfare protection. But Denmark sets a good example in areas such as energy efficiency and donations of **aid** to developing countries.

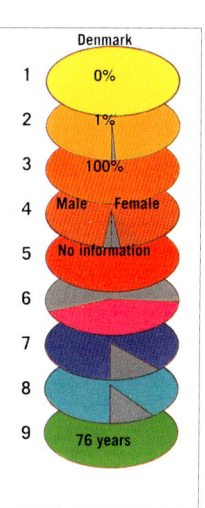

HAVES AND HAVE-NOTS: HUMAN NEEDS AND HUMAN RIGHTS
Millions of people suffer a lack of one or more of the essential requirements for a decent life, most of which are interconnected. Clean water, a safe environment, protection from violence, and equality of opportunity are everyone's right. The numbered bands on the globe represent other key human needs or rights. The lighter shaded area at the right-hand side of each band shows the **percentage** of the world's **population** whose needs are met and who enjoy adequate rights. The darker shaded area at the left-hand side shows the proportion of people whose needs or rights are unfulfilled.

HUMANKIND

WORLD AT WORK

What job would you like to have when you are older? Like most people, you probably hope to combine reasonably good earnings with doing something worthwhile and useful. Worldwide, however, few people can be sure of a satisfying and well-paid job for life. Advances in technology and changes of government policy mean that the jobs market is changing fast.

THE HUMAN RESOURCE
The ways in which human skills and energy are used are affected by the numbers of people in the workforce and how quickly they increase, the proportions of men and women in the workforce, the changing nature of work, and how we value work – whether it is paid or unpaid, for example. There are great differences between regions of the developed world (right) and those of the developing world (far right). Workforces are expanding much more slowly in developed countries, and women make up a larger proportion of paid workers. Every region of the world, however, is being affected by major changes in work practices.

Work was once simply what people did to survive: **hunting and gathering**, farming; making tools and shelter; learning, teaching, and practising skills. Even after trade and money first developed, most work was based on farming.

Since the **Industrial Revolution**, work moved from fields to factories and offices – although millions of people, mainly in developing countries, still live by farming and fishing. Work has come more and more to mean having a paid job. We sometimes forget there are many people who work but are not in paid jobs.

The spread of labour-saving technologies has affected employment, resulting in job losses in traditional **industries**. On the plus side, electronics, wholesale and retail selling, **service industries** such as leisure, and other industries have created **white-collar** (non-manual, office-type) jobs.

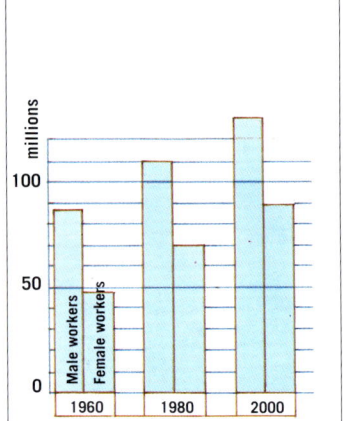

In North America, Japan, and Oceania more and more women are entering a steadily expanding workforce.

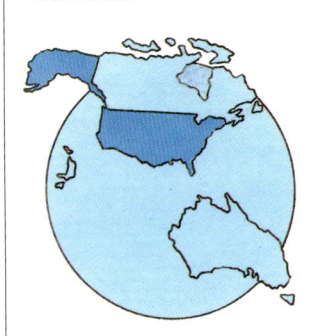

The United States has seen a loss of farm-based work, especially on smaller farms, and **blue-collar work** (manual jobs in industry). White-collar (office-type) employment in services such as finance and in government has expanded.

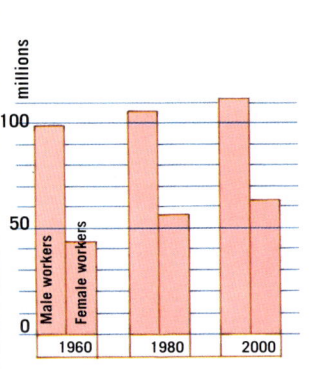

Western Europe has a slow-growing workforce. Women's share of paid work is increasing, but only gradually.

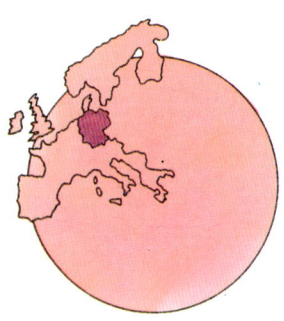

Germany has the strongest economy in Europe, despite problems caused by uniting with poorer East Germany in 1990. Like the USA, Germany has lost jobs in agriculture and heavy industry and gained them in services.

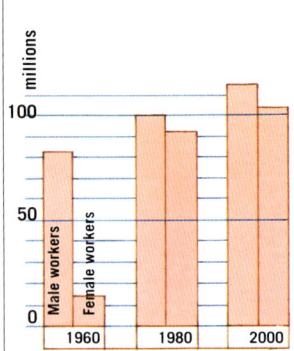

Eastern Europe and the former USSR now have almost as many women as men in work, a huge change since 1960.

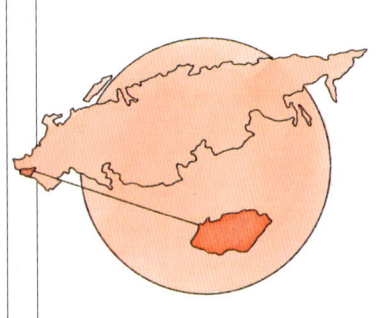

Hungary has one of the more successful economies of the former **communist** countries of Eastern Europe. Many new industrial jobs have developed, although farm work has declined. Women make up almost half the workforce.

At the same time, more women have gone out to work – although many of them part-time, and often as cheap labour. In developing countries fast-rising populations are perhaps the main factor affecting the jobs market.

The global workforce is growing by about 50 million people a year. The challenge for the future is to ensure that the work most worth doing gets done, while every adult has a decent job and a fair income.

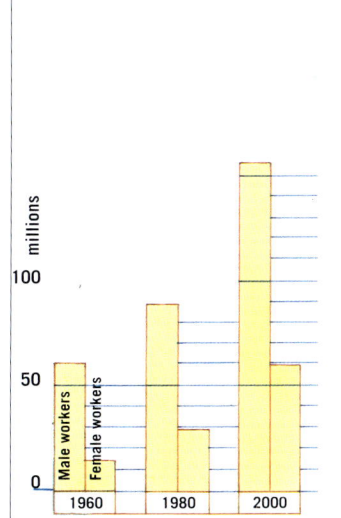

In Latin America and the Caribbean the paid workforce has always contained more than twice as many men as women.

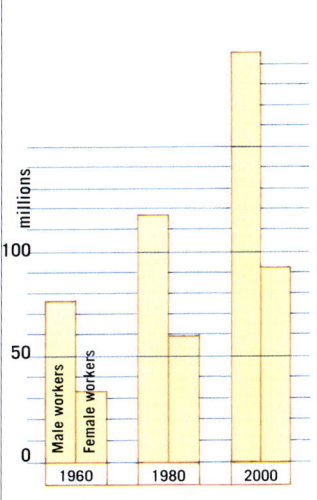

Africa's share of paid female to male workers has stayed steady since 1960. Yet millions of unpaid women farmers support their families.

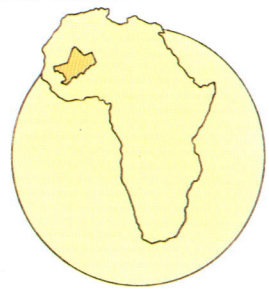

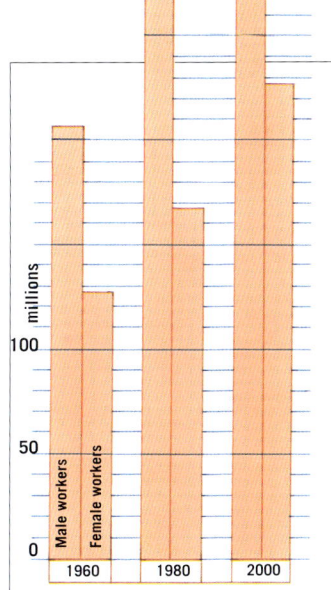

East Asia, including China, has a large and rapidly growing workforce. About 40 per cent of East Asian workers are women.

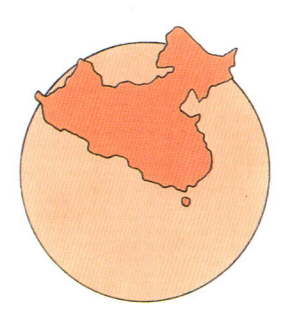

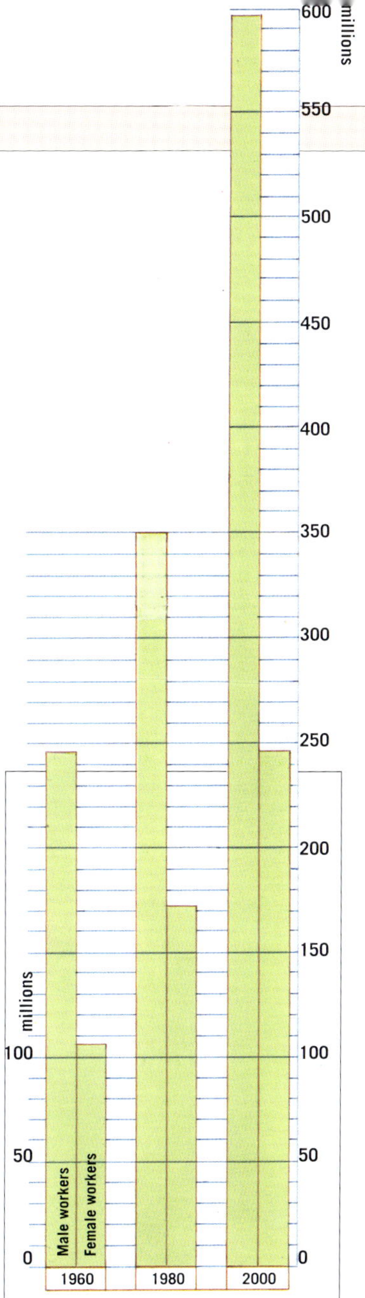

South and Southeast Asia has a fast-rising population and the world's largest workforce. Men far outnumber women in the jobs market.

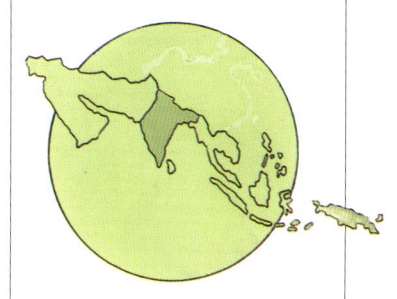

Brazil is the economic giant of South America, with employment growing in industry and services. But rising poverty has led to a huge increase in the numbers of city slum dwellers doing very low-paid casual work.

Mali is poor but has little unemployment because most Malians support themselves as small-scale farmers. Modernization of agriculture could help the country's industry to develop but may lead to serious unemployment.

China has an enormous population that is still based mainly in peasant farming communities. Job opportunities are in towns and cities, where factory work is increasing and industries producing goods for export are expanding.

India has a larger population than any country except China. More than two-thirds of its people depend on the land, many of them as self-employed farmers. Its workforce looks set to be the world's largest by the year 2040.

HUMANKIND

CLEVER OR WISE?

Being clever is not the same as being intelligent. A cunning thief who climbs through a window and steals a camera, for example, may realize later that his actions were not wise. We have put much of our human cleverness to good use, and we call ourselves *Homo sapiens* – "wise man" – but there is still room for improvement.

Children in Simiatug, in the highlands of Ecuador, learn to read in Quechua, the traditional language of the Andean peoples.

Unlike other animal species, we can transform our environment. The history of human **development** is one of impressive achievement based on knowledge and skill: towns and cities, farms and factories, mighty machines and beautiful buildings, and great art.

With knowledge comes the need to learn. More people can read and write than ever before, and almost three-quarters of the world's children are in school. We build more universities and publish more books than ever, while newspapers, radio, and television reach their largest-ever audiences. We spend more money than ever on developing new technologies, although many of these are for military purposes.

Even so, millions of people worldwide still lack schooling and access to modern information channels. A decent life is possible without literacy or schooling but difficult to achieve. **Illiterate** people are more likely to suffer poverty and ill-health, for example.

But more does not always mean better. Modern Western science and learning are sometimes too highly specialized to affect human well-being. Education does not always lead to an understanding of the best way to solve real-life problems. And we have neglected the wisdom of traditional communities such as rainforest peoples.

Many people believe we need to close the gaps that separate science from art, modern knowledge from old-fashioned intelligence, high technology from everyday usefulness, and information-rich people in developed countries from their information-poor cousins in the developing world.

The information gap

We rely on **information technology** and the media to tell us about the modern world. Most people who use these live in the developed world, but developing countries need them just as much.

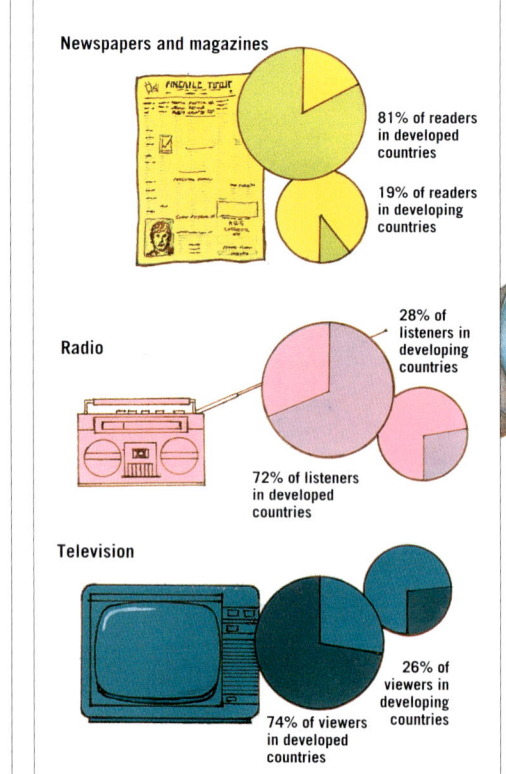

Newspapers and magazines
- 81% of readers in developed countries
- 19% of readers in developing countries

Radio
- 28% of listeners in developing countries
- 72% of listeners in developed countries

Television
- 26% of viewers in developing countries
- 74% of viewers in developed countries

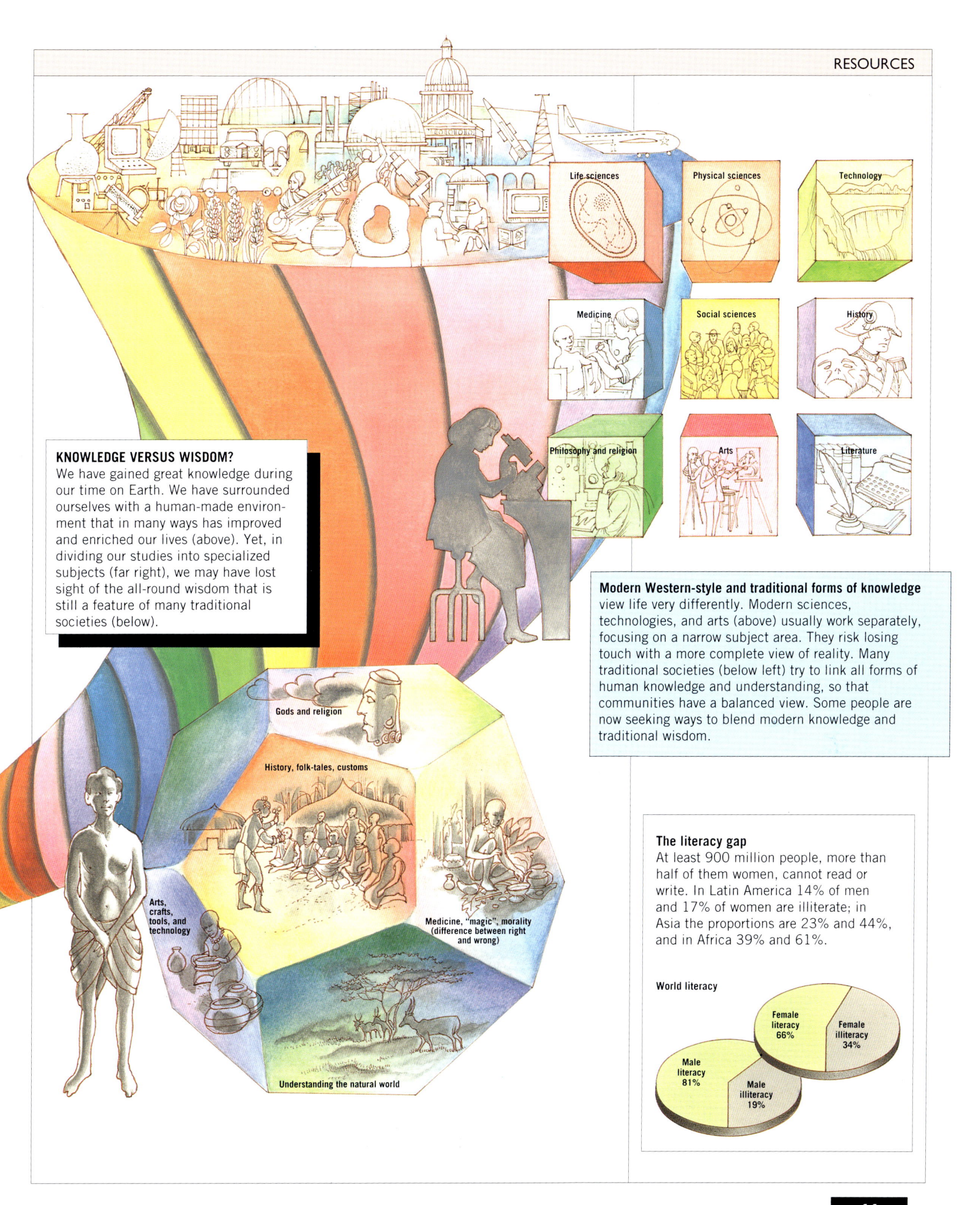

RESOURCES

KNOWLEDGE VERSUS WISDOM?
We have gained great knowledge during our time on Earth. We have surrounded ourselves with a human-made environment that in many ways has improved and enriched our lives (above). Yet, in dividing our studies into specialized subjects (far right), we may have lost sight of the all-round wisdom that is still a feature of many traditional societies (below).

Modern Western-style and traditional forms of knowledge view life very differently. Modern sciences, technologies, and arts (above) usually work separately, focusing on a narrow subject area. They risk losing touch with a more complete view of reality. Many traditional societies (below left) try to link all forms of human knowledge and understanding, so that communities have a balanced view. Some people are now seeking ways to blend modern knowledge and traditional wisdom.

The literacy gap
At least 900 million people, more than half of them women, cannot read or write. In Latin America 14% of men and 17% of women are illiterate; in Asia the proportions are 23% and 44%, and in Africa 39% and 61%.

World literacy

Female literacy 66%
Female illiteracy 34%
Male literacy 81%
Male illiteracy 19%

11

HUMANKIND

PEOPLE & HEALTH

In the time it takes to count from 1 to 60, 180 babies are born, and 25 children aged five or under die. Most of these births and deaths take place in developing countries. The birth of a baby and growth of a child should bring great joy, but hunger, sickness, poverty, and death dominate the lives of many parents in the developing world. Are we doing enough to put this right?

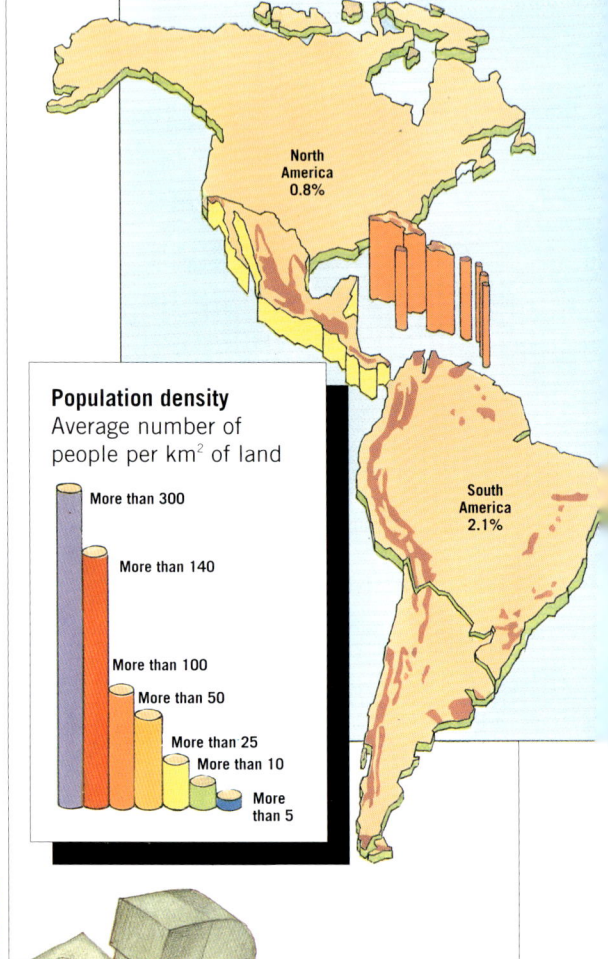

DID YOU KNOW?

A question of priorities
Since 1945, 620 million people, up to a third of them children, have died from lack of food, safe water, and basic health care – 28 times more than have died as a result of war. Yet many countries spend four times more money on armies and weapons than they do on health (including birth control). In East Africa there is only one doctor for every 60,000 people, and the average person in most of Africa dies 24 years younger than the average North American or Western European.

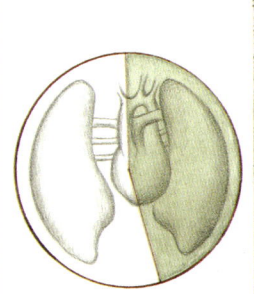

The world population is increasing by 90–100 million a year. Africa has the fastest growth rate and will double its population in 23 years.

Why are numbers rising so fast? Modern health care has reduced **mortality rates**, so more people live longer. **Birth rates** have risen in many developing countries as industrialization changes traditional communities. Women often lack adequate birth control, and poor people see children as useful workers and produce more in the hope that at least some of them will survive.

Developed countries take more than their fair share of resources. Rich countries **import** much of their food from hungry Africa, Asia, and Latin America.

Population density
Average number of people per km² of land

- More than 300
- More than 140
- More than 100
- More than 50
- More than 25
- More than 10
- More than 5

North America 0.8%

South America 2.1%

New illnesses, some of them the result of people having wealthier lifestyles, include cancer, heart disease, and **AIDS**, which is spreading at a rate of a million new cases a year.

Mental and emotional illness affects more than 40 million people worldwide. We spend a lot of money on treatments to relieve stress, but many of them bring their own problems, such as addiction.

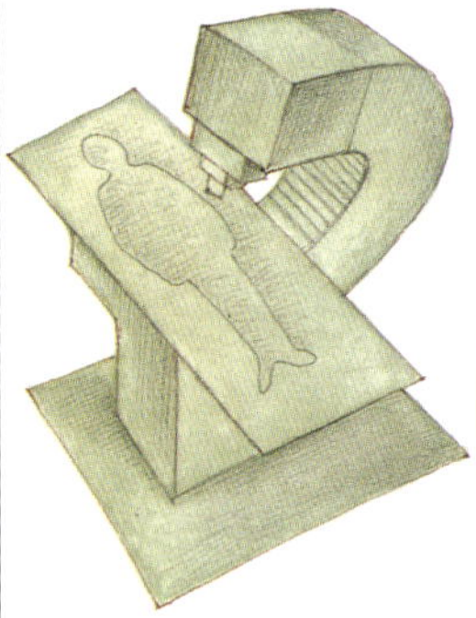

High-technology medicine is costly and cures only a few known diseases. In developing countries especially, money spent on simpler ways of preventing illness benefits many more people.

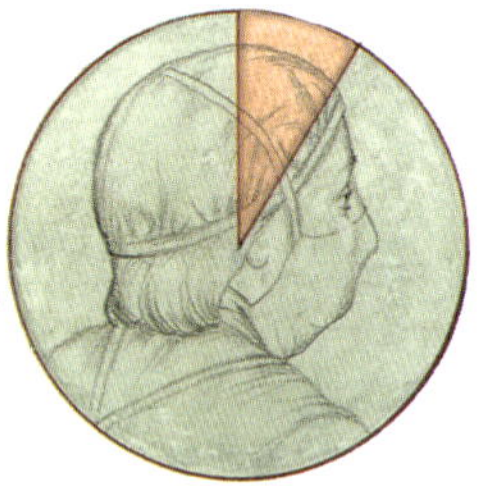

Health-care budgets vary enormously. Developed countries, which have smaller populations and fewer health problems, spend ten times more on health overall than developing countries.

6000 BC   5000 BC   4000 BC   3000 BC

PROBLEMS

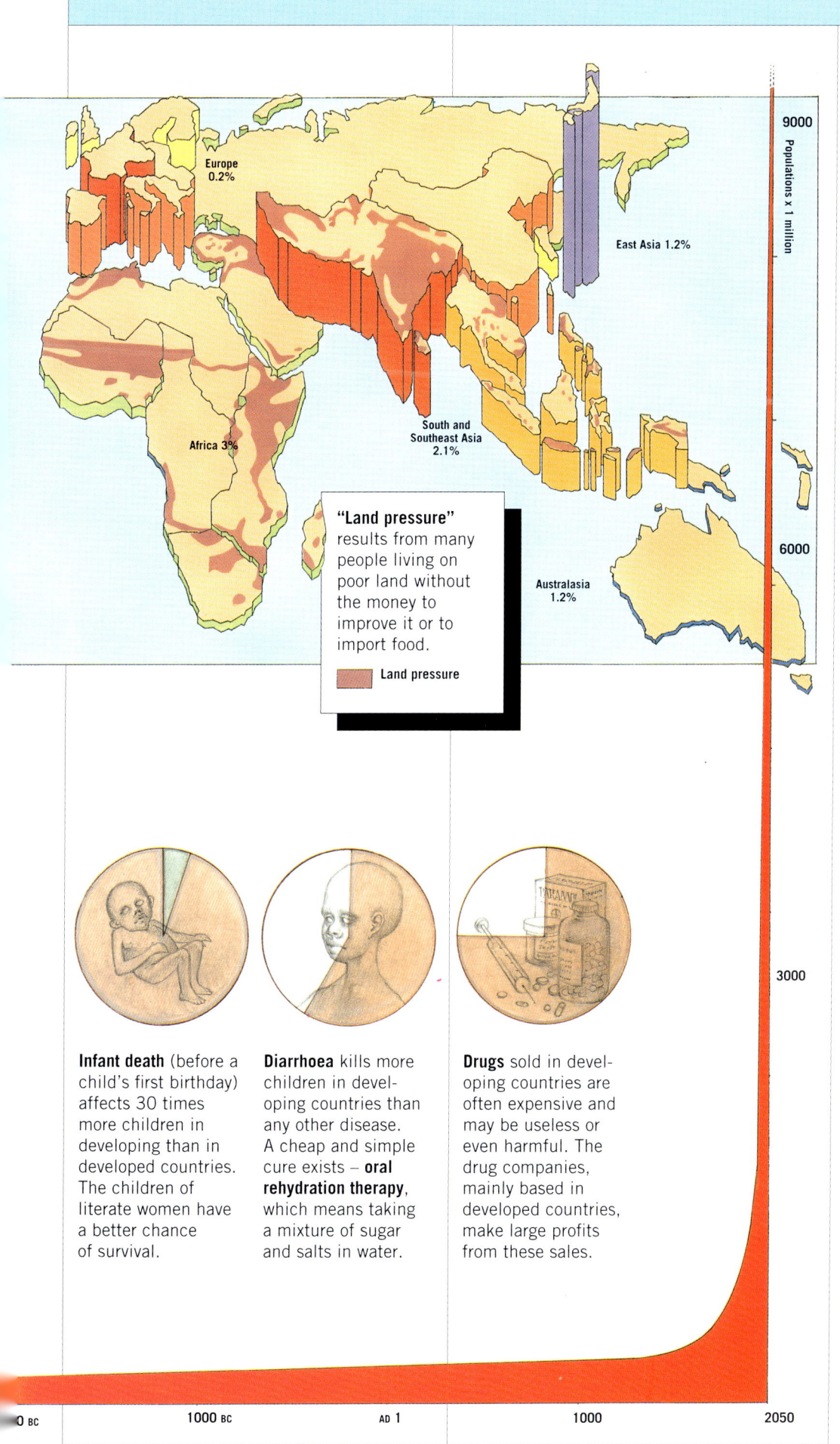

High- and low-population regions and population growth
The map shows regional rates of population growth, population density, and areas where large numbers of people, poor land, and low incomes threaten hunger, ill-health, and worsening poverty.

Better health care
Millions of people die each year from **malnutrition** (poor diet) and preventable **infections**. About 900 million people in developing countries have few medical services, and many millions lack education in basic hygiene.

Poisoned environments are an increasing cause of illness, especially in the countries of the former Soviet Union and Eastern Europe, where industrial development has been badly managed. Much of the water in these countries is unfit to drink, and millions are at risk from **cancer**, asthma, birth defects, and mental illness.

We spend much more money coping with illness than preventing it. Larger budgets for health education and other forms of prevention in developed countries could reduce heart disease, stress, alcoholism, drug addiction, and cancer deaths from smoking. More spending on health care for women and children and on birth control in developing countries could also bring about major improvements.

Population explosion?
Human numbers increased slowly for thousands of years, but then that increase accelerated dramatically. There were 1000 million people alive by the year 1800, 2000 million by 1935, 3000 million by 1960, 4000 million by 1974, 5000 million by 1987. An end-of-century total of more than 6000 million is certain, rising to perhaps 9000 million or more by the year 2050.

Europe 0.2%
East Asia 1.2%
Africa 3%
South and Southeast Asia 2.1%
Australasia 1.2%

"Land pressure" results from many people living on poor land without the money to improve it or to import food.

Land pressure

Populations x 1 million — 9000, 6000, 3000

0 BC — 1000 BC — AD 1 — 1000 — 2050

Infant death (before a child's first birthday) affects 30 times more children in developing than in developed countries. The children of literate women have a better chance of survival.

Diarrhoea kills more children in developing countries than any other disease. A cheap and simple cure exists – **oral rehydration therapy**, which means taking a mixture of sugar and salts in water.

Drugs sold in developing countries are often expensive and may be useless or even harmful. The drug companies, mainly based in developed countries, make large profits from these sales.

13

HUMANKIND

OUT OF WORK

Millions of adults who are willing to work cannot find useful jobs. Unemployment has badly hit developed countries since the mid-1970s, despite some new job opportunities. Governments could create many more jobs by taxing pollution and the use of resources.

Developed countries saw their unemployment rates double between 1973 and 1988. During periods of economic difficulty, industries reduced their workforces, closed down altogether, or moved to developing countries where labour was cheaper.

Being out of work means more than not earning money, as any adult who has lost their job will tell you. It can make a person feel frustrated or a complete failure. Worse than this, in poor countries where there are few welfare provisions, people who lose their livelihood and cannot support themselves or their families risk losing everything, perhaps even life itself.

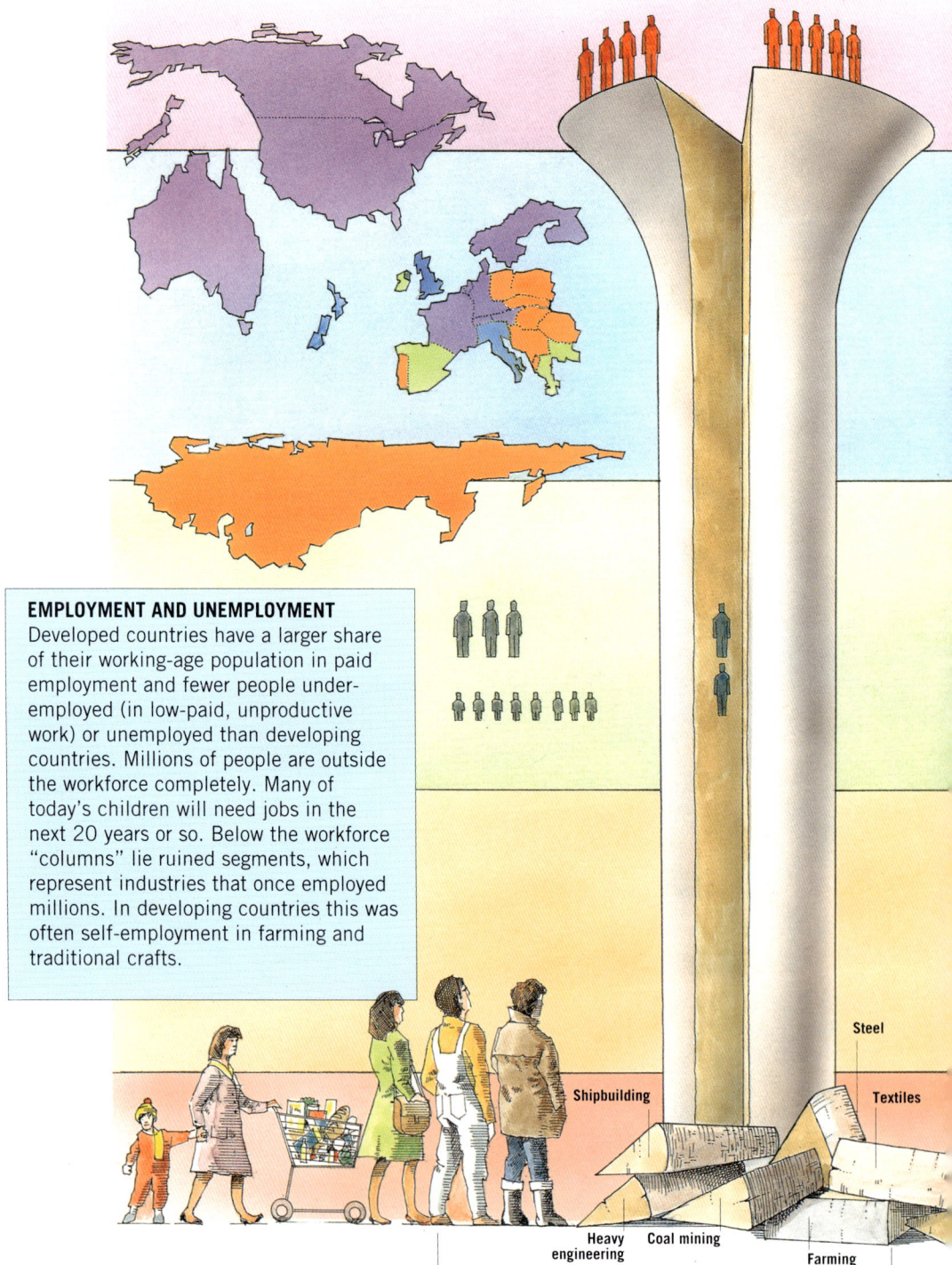

Whole families live and work on Aroma, the main rubbish dump for the sprawling city of Manila in the Philippines. They collect anything that can be recycled – glass, plastic, fabric, or scrap metal – and sell it to survive.

EMPLOYMENT AND UNEMPLOYMENT
Developed countries have a larger share of their working-age population in paid employment and fewer people under-employed (in low-paid, unproductive work) or unemployed than developing countries. Millions of people are outside the workforce completely. Many of today's children will need jobs in the next 20 years or so. Below the workforce "columns" lie ruined segments, which represent industries that once employed millions. In developing countries this was often self-employment in farming and traditional crafts.

Developed countries
80% of working-age population in paid jobs

Steel
Shipbuilding
Textiles
Heavy engineering
Coal mining
Farming

14

PROBLEMS

In developing countries most people were once farmers, fisher-people, craft workers, or traders. Paid work has always been in short supply. But age-old ways of life are under threat, often because big business has taken over the land. Fast-rising populations worsen the problem. The result has been a massive movement of people from countryside to city.

Not enough new jobs are to be found in the expanding cities of developing countries, however. In desperation, many people join the **informal economy** of casual and sometimes illegal work, where nobody keeps records or pays tax, and income is uncertain. Such work might be in street trading, rubbish **recycling**, or other, often unhealthy, areas of unofficial employment. Tragically, some people take advantage of children, employing them in factories or as prostitutes.

People seeking work also migrate to developed countries. The USA and Western Europe used to welcome unskilled migrants as low-paid workers – such as Turkish workers in Germany in the 1960s – but no longer do so.

Some groups are less successful than others in the jobs market. Many women and members of **ethnic minorities** find it hard to enter some better-paid occupations or achieve senior levels in others.

Yet there is more to work than paid jobs. Women still grow a huge share of the world's food for home and village **consumption**, and do most housework, including the collection of water and **fuelwood** in developing countries. They receive no payment for this work.

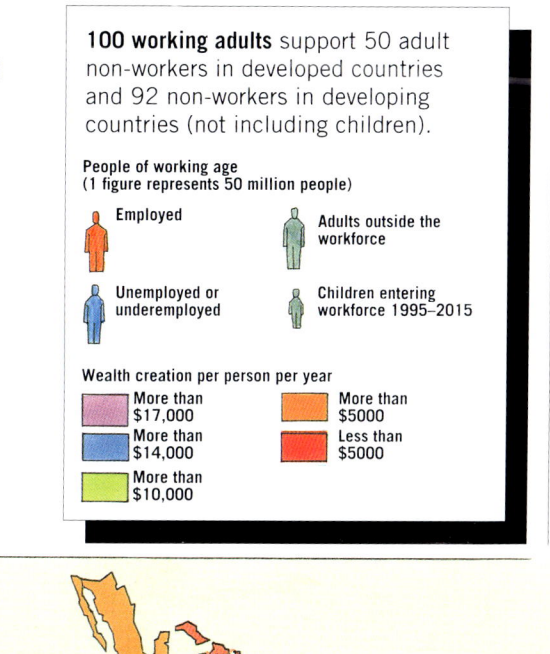

Developed countries have lost many jobs in traditional industries such as shipbuilding since the 1970s. Fewer jobs in services and other areas have been created.

Developing countries have many more low-paid or unpaid jobs than well-paid ones, for example in farming; few welfare schemes; and millions of people who scrape a living.

Developing countries
64% of working-age population in paid jobs

100 working adults support 50 adult non-workers in developed countries and 92 non-workers in developing countries (not including children).

People of working age
(1 figure represents 50 million people)

- Employed
- Adults outside the workforce
- Unemployed or underemployed
- Children entering workforce 1995–2015

Wealth creation per person per year
- More than $17,000
- More than $14,000
- More than $10,000
- More than $5000
- Less than $5000

Traditional crafts

Farming   Sugar   Jute

15

HUMANKIND

RIGHTS IN CRISIS

Children often say "It's not fair", and their protest may well be about a silly, unimportant issue. But unfairness can be serious, as when a bigger child harms a smaller one. Bullying goes on among adults too: stronger groups of people mistreat weaker ones, sometimes with great cruelty. Is there anything we can do to help make the world a fairer place?

Rwandan refugees live in camps in the Karagwe district of Tanzania. Aid agencies help provide food and health care. Up to ten people live in a brende, a wooden-framed shelter with walls made from reeds or mud and a plastic sheet for a roof.

The 1948 United Nations Declaration of Human Rights aims to guarantee people everywhere a decent standard of living, the right to education and equality in law, the freedom to hold opinions and speak without fear, and freedom from violence and oppression. But for millions of people – including women, children, minority groups, and those with unjust rulers – these rights and freedoms mean little. In many developing countries women have fewer rights than men. Some societies prevent women from owning land, for example, or think it natural to treat boys better than girls and for men to control and mistreat women. Violence against women is a problem almost everywhere.

Children suffer when poverty denies them education or forces them into work, sometimes as slaves. In many countries homeless youngsters live on city streets, begging, stealing, or taking drugs: many die young. Others are the victims of war, made to fight (as young as ten), or killed by adults.

THE REFUGEE CRISIS
There are about 23 million refugees across the world, living in foreign countries, often separated from their families, and usually in poverty. Millions more people have been forced away from their homes but remain in their own country. The map shows refugee populations at the start of the 1990s, before the impact of the conflicts in Rwanda and the former Yugoslavia. (Palestinian refugees are not shown.)

Number of refugees living in each country, early 1990s

- More than 1,000,000
- More than 500,000
- More than 100,000
- More than 50,000
- More than 10,000
- Less than 10,000
- → Movement of refugees
- ★ Areas of major conflict
- Areas threatened by famine

PROBLEMS

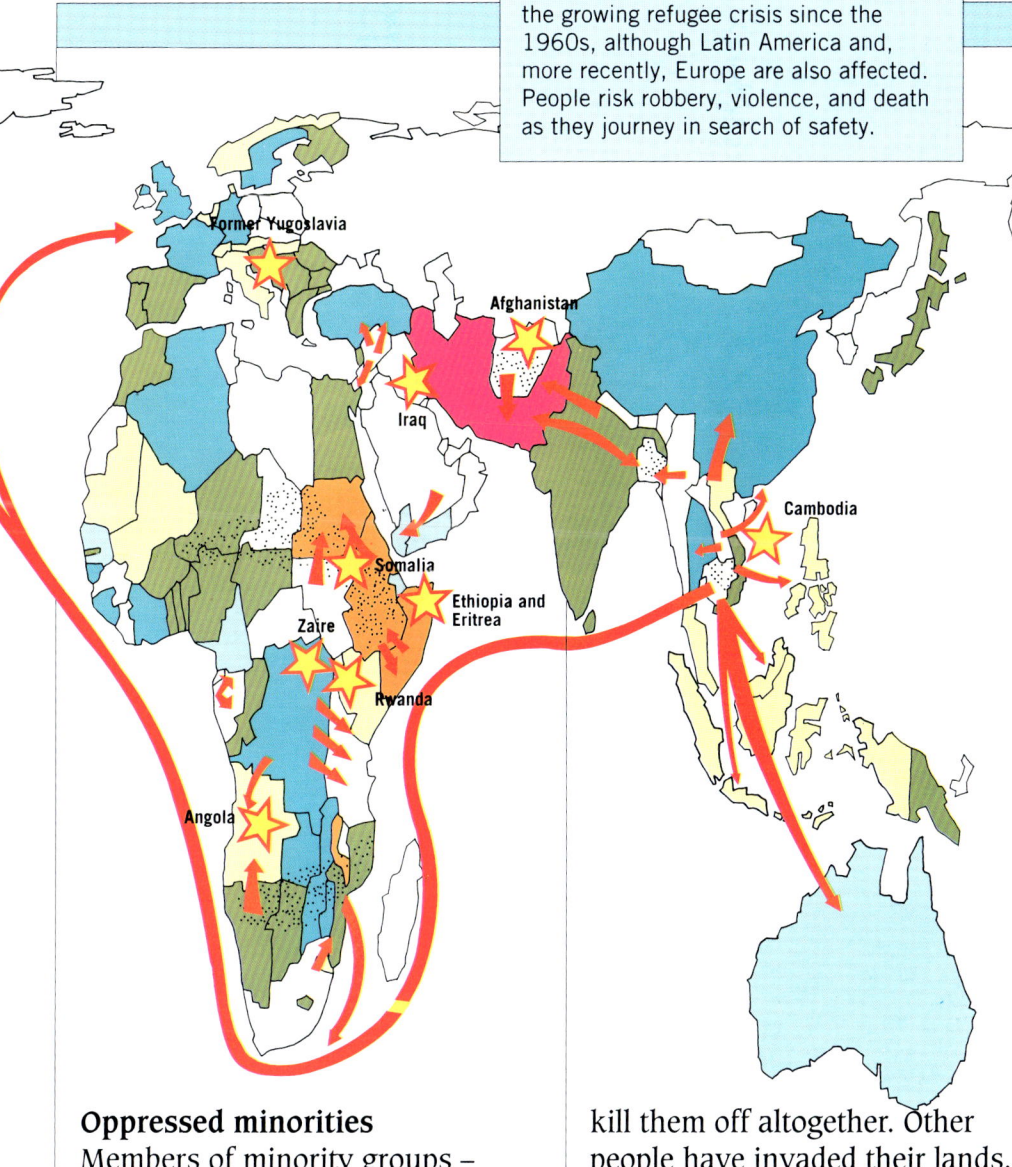

Africa and Asia have suffered most from the growing refugee crisis since the 1960s, although Latin America and, more recently, Europe are also affected. People risk robbery, violence, and death as they journey in search of safety.

benefit from a world system of trade and **communication** that makes some people rich and powerful and others poor and weak. Their governments sometimes support violent rulers if it suits them, for the sake of trade agreements for example, or else they may not deal adequately with the poor treatment of their own minority groups.

Millions of people whose human rights are denied become **refugees**, leaving their countries in search of a better chance of survival elsewhere. Most refugees, half of whom are children, live in developing countries, often in unhealthy and overcrowded camps or slums. Sudden movements of refugees can cause environmental crises when lots of people overwhelm local facilities. Others, unable to escape, suffer poverty and persecution in their own countries.

But the picture is not hopeless. With the end of **apartheid** in South Africa in 1993–94, for example, the black population emerged from decades of suffering to face a hopeful future.

Oppressed minorities

Members of minority groups – people who are different from the majority of the population in their religion, language, **culture**, or ethnic background – often do not enjoy the full range of freedoms and rights that the majority do. Some minorities cannot practise their religion openly or at all, are trapped in poverty because they are discriminated against throughout society, or they lose control over their traditional lands.

The world's 250 million **indigenous people** (the original inhabitants of a region), including the rainforest tribes, have suffered terrible injustice and cruelty. Some settlers and governments have tried to destroy their way of life or kill them off altogether. Other people have invaded their lands, often bringing "development" in the shape of logging, big-business farming, dams, and mines. Many indigenous peoples have organized themselves to demand their rights.

The rule of tyrants

A lack of democracy in some developing countries, such as China, means that rulers mistreat their citizens, imposing unjust laws. Human rights groups have thousands of files listing the wrongful arrest, torture, imprisonment, disappearance, and killing of innocent people.

Developed countries are also involved in the human rights crisis. They have established and

HOME ACTION

Help improve human rights worldwide.
- Treat people fairly, whatever their background or origins.
- Complain when somebody is mistreated.
- Support calls for better rights for people with disabilities.
- Support women's organizations, such as those working for equal opportunities.
- Buy **fair-traded** goods.
- Write to newspapers, magazines, and your representative in government about human rights problems.
- Join a human rights organization such as Amnesty International, the Minority Rights Group, or Survival International.

GAIA WATCH

THE MACUXI OF BRAZIL

"There used to be a lot of game here: deer, armadillos, anteaters, capybara, ducks. We used to hunt them with bows and arrows and with rifles. I was a good shot with a bow and arrow . . . but now it's all gone, and nowadays even fish are difficult to find. Everything got bad when the ranchers came in. The river used to be very clear in the summer: now it's just as muddy as it is in the winter, in the rainy season."

Ricardo Nascimento remembers how life used to be for the Macuxi people, who live near the River Mau, a tributary of the Branco, in northern Brazil. For many years their way of life has been under threat. Cattle ranchers are buying up what was traditionally Macuxi land, and gold miners are polluting the rivers with mercury. But politicians tell the Macuxi that they have to change to be part of the new Brazil.

▲ **The River Mau** lies on Brazil's northwestern border with Guyana. Mining for gold and diamonds began here on a small scale in the 1930s, but by the early 1990s hundreds of miners were extracting gold from the river bed. The local community of Macuxi Indians, who have lived here for generations, resented the miners' invasion. They organized a campaign to evict them from the land. Although the gold miners have now gone, "scars" remain along the river banks.

▶ **The activites of the gold miners** polluted the river, killing fish, and drove away some of the wildlife of a region originally rich in plant and animal life.

Lindalva Nascimento, whose daughter is a health worker, says: "In the past, our children were not taught at school about our Macuxi customs – the herbs we used for medicines, the prayers of the *pajes* (doctor-priests) – and they were lost. Now we want to go back to them: it's not easy, but we have begun. Now my daughter and the other health workers are learning how to make potions and creams, and how to prescribe traditional herbal treatments for things like toothache and earache."

Geronimo de Oliviera teaches maths at Siminyo school, the largest school in the Macuxi territory. "The school is important because our children learn to read and write in their own language. It is vital for rescuing our culture. It all began when the *tuaxas* (community leaders) decided it was wrong to be ashamed of our culture, to have no more dancing and singing. Of course there were problems – there were no books. We had to write all the materials: we have even written books of Macuxi legends."

"The politicians say we want to return to the past," says Geronimo, "that we aren't Indian any more; that we are standing in the way of progress. But we are not. We just want our rights to be respected. We want to be seen as human beings, of a different culture."

▼ **Health workers** are learning how to make tinctures (medicinal preparations), creams, and herbal remedies so they can treat people according to traditional Macuxi methods. The most common complaints are diarrhoea, influenza, and toothache. There has been malaria too since the miners came.

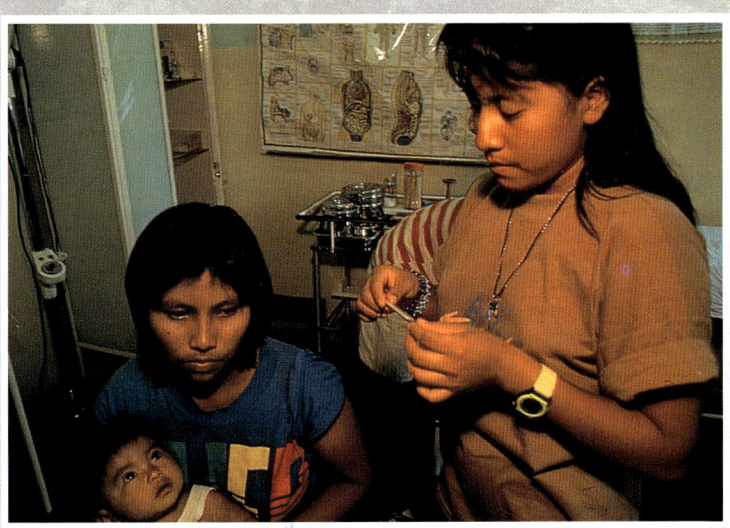

▼ **Macuxi students** can now learn their own language, and about their culture and history, as part of their formal education. Knowledge and stories from the past were not being passed on from generation to generation, but now efforts are being made to keep that knowledge alive within the Macuxi community.

HUMANKIND

BETTER HEALTH

Your parents may have often told you to wash your hands before meals and to brush your teeth afterwards. These chores can be a nuisance when you're in a hurry. But if you got food poisoning or a raging toothache you would realize that prevention is better than cure. And that's the message of family planning and primary health care too.

Managing human numbers is essential if health is to improve. To reduce birth rates women need access to well-run **family planning** services, more opportunities for education (literate women have fewer, healthier children), and better welfare provision. Greater equality between rich and poor, and between women and men, usually results in smaller families.

China, Colombia, Cuba, Kerala state in India, Singapore, Sri Lanka, and Tunisia all reduced birth rates in the 1960s and 1970s by promoting birth control, and improving child health and the social position of women. Government policies encouraged small families with tax relief, pensions, and other schemes.

An international effort could bring the projected world population figure of 9000–10,000 million by 2050 down to 8500 million.

▶ **Community health workers** bridge the gap between government services and the people. They can help identify sickness early and advise people on healthier ways of living.

▶ **Regular check-ups** not only improve personal health but save money by detecting illness at the start, when treatment is often less expensive than at a later stage.

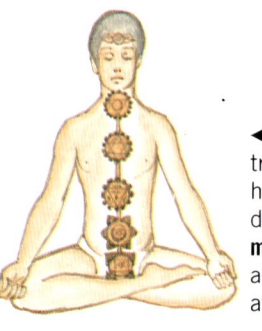

◀ **"Alternative" medicine,** based on traditional treatments such as acupuncture, yoga, and herbal remedies, is growing in popularity in developed countries. **Complementary medicine,** drawing on both conventional and alternative treatments, is also receiving more attention from medical professionals.

Primary health care for all
Primary health care services use links between health workers and the community to prevent illness or treat it as early as possible. Mother and child health is a key aspect of this. People in both developed and developing countries benefit from primary health care. The defence of health is symbolized by the snakes and rod of the Roman god of healing, Aesculapius.

Developed countries have successful primary health care programmes. These programmes have helped reduce infant deaths and hospital admissions. Public education campaigns in Scandinavia promoting healthier lifestyles have led to lower rates of tooth decay, cancer, and deaths from heart disease.

Developed country

Community hospital/health centre

Community health workers

Self-help groups

Early detection of health problems

▲ **Self-help groups** allow women to plan their families better, and help people overcome health problems such as alcoholism, drug addiction, depression, and physical disability.

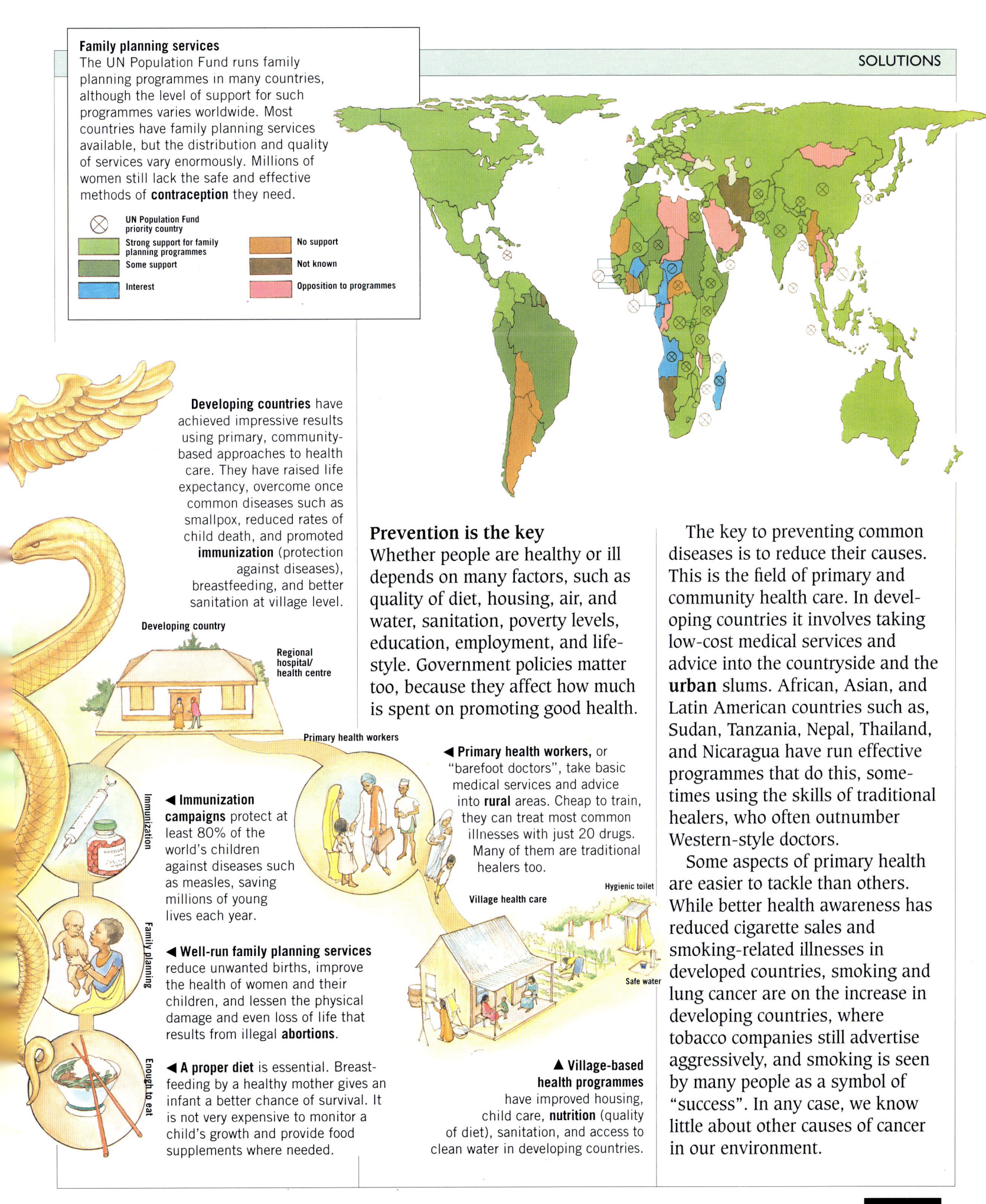

SOLUTIONS

Family planning services
The UN Population Fund runs family planning programmes in many countries, although the level of support for such programmes varies worldwide. Most countries have family planning services available, but the distribution and quality of services vary enormously. Millions of women still lack the safe and effective methods of **contraception** they need.

- ⊗ UN Population Fund priority country
- Strong support for family planning programmes
- Some support
- Interest
- No support
- Not known
- Opposition to programmes

Developing countries have achieved impressive results using primary, community-based approaches to health care. They have raised life expectancy, overcome once common diseases such as smallpox, reduced rates of child death, and promoted **immunization** (protection against diseases), breastfeeding, and better sanitation at village level.

◀ **Immunization campaigns** protect at least 80% of the world's children against diseases such as measles, saving millions of young lives each year.

◀ **Well-run family planning services** reduce unwanted births, improve the health of women and their children, and lessen the physical damage and even loss of life that results from illegal **abortions**.

◀ **A proper diet** is essential. Breastfeeding by a healthy mother gives an infant a better chance of survival. It is not very expensive to monitor a child's growth and provide food supplements where needed.

◀ **Primary health workers**, or "barefoot doctors", take basic medical services and advice into **rural** areas. Cheap to train, they can treat most common illnesses with just 20 drugs. Many of them are traditional healers too.

▲ **Village-based health programmes** have improved housing, child care, **nutrition** (quality of diet), sanitation, and access to clean water in developing countries.

Prevention is the key
Whether people are healthy or ill depends on many factors, such as quality of diet, housing, air, and water, sanitation, poverty levels, education, employment, and lifestyle. Government policies matter too, because they affect how much is spent on promoting good health.

The key to preventing common diseases is to reduce their causes. This is the field of primary and community health care. In developing countries it involves taking low-cost medical services and advice into the countryside and the **urban** slums. African, Asian, and Latin American countries such as, Sudan, Tanzania, Nepal, Thailand, and Nicaragua have run effective programmes that do this, sometimes using the skills of traditional healers, who often outnumber Western-style doctors.

Some aspects of primary health are easier to tackle than others. While better health awareness has reduced cigarette sales and smoking-related illnesses in developed countries, smoking and lung cancer are on the increase in developing countries, where tobacco companies still advertise aggressively, and smoking is seen by many people as a symbol of "success". In any case, we know little about other causes of cancer in our environment.

HUMANKIND

SHARING SKILLS

The problems we face need community-wide solutions. While millions of people lack paid work, an enormous range of worthwhile tasks need doing. These include cleaning up polluted sites; planting trees; producing food and energy in an environmentally friendly way; building low-cost housing; repairing and recycling; bringing health and education services to villages and **inner-city** slums in developing countries; and caring for older people and those with disabilities. All over the world people are working together in communities to improve the quality of life for everyone. Government policies often help but sometimes hinder this work.

Community education means using schools and colleges for the whole community – not just for training for jobs. People of all ages welcome the opportunity to learn new skills, extend their knowledge, and find new ways to manage their lives.

WORKING AS A COMMUNITY: THE KEY TO PROGRESS
All round the world people are working together locally and globally to solve problems. Community groups are not perfect, and there are sometimes problems between members. But successful "**grass-roots**" efforts show that it is possible to overcome poverty, unemployment, physical health problems, and lack of education, to protect and improve local environments, and to make societies more fair and equal through peaceful social and political change.

Suppose that each of us has a broken bicycle. You know how to fix a bike but don't have any tools; I am no good at mending things but I have got a box of spanners and spares. If we won't talk to each other we're stuck. But by sharing our skills and resources, working as a team, or community, we might end up with two working bikes.

Low-cost technologies and good communications are important in developing countries. Organizations promoting **intermediate technology** help local people set up small-scale community businesses (below). Satellites are used to bring much-needed information to the poor in the countryside (right).

Fair-trade organizations help producer **co-operatives** in developing countries **export** their produce to the developed world for decent prices. A growing network of **non-governmental organizations** (**NGOs**) and human rights groups are working to make co-operation the basis of the way we go about **commercial** business.

DID YOU KNOW?

Trade without money
Local Exchange Trading Systems, or **LETS**, are a new and popular form of community action. Members of a LETS system use each other's skills and services – from babysitting to house building – but pay in "local currency", that is, each other's services, not cash. A central computer prints a monthly statement showing what each person has "bought" and "sold". People using LETS find that their quality of life improves, while their cash spending decreases. Hundreds of groups are now running in Western Europe, North America, and Australasia.

SOLUTIONS

Distance learning is a method of home-based study, based on telephone and postal communication, radio, television, and computers, as well as books.

Number of distance-learning students
- More than 500,000
- More than 100,000
- Less than 100,000
- Not known
- ● Major distance-learning organization

Community co-operatives take many forms: farming, fishing, craft, building, industrial, marketing, and other worker co-operatives, women's groups, housing associations, and joint savings and credit schemes. Hundreds of thousands of people have set up or joined co-operatives and found them a valuable way of overcoming problems.

Television and radio broadcasting can be a powerful force for good in helping people improve their lives. The much-loved children's television programme *Sesame Street*, for example, teaches literacy, numeracy, personal health, tolerance, and self-respect, all with a sense of fun. Many countries show similar programmes.

Communities often lack money, productive land, or other resources, and need outside help. Governments and non-governmental organizations such as Oxfam, have provided funding, legal protection, advice, training, and equipment for **reforestation** (left), building programmes (right) and other projects, and not just in developing countries.

Derelict sites in towns and cities can be used by local people to establish new businesses (left), or new neighbourhood resources, such as parks and gardens (right). Community improvements are usually most successful when local people have control over decisions, and benefit directly from new job opportunities that are created.

Agenda 21
Governments attending the UN **Earth Summit** in Rio de Janeiro, Brazil, in 1992, reached several agreements. **Agenda 21** is a programme of action for **sustainable development** – in other words, a plan for improving people's quality of life everywhere in the world without damaging the environment or resources.

23

CIVILIZATION

"The only war we seek should be . . . against humankind's ancient enemies – poverty, hunger, illiteracy, and preventable disease . . . . Poor people, women, youth, the disabled, older people… we are all in this together."

PETRA KELLY,
leader of Germany's Green movement, who died in 1992

Civilization: what a splendid word! It sums up everything that human beings can be proud of. We can boast of many magnificent achievements in the past and more recently; and there will be more in the future. But let's be honest. We have built a lot more slums than palaces and cathedrals; at least as many people have died in poverty around the world as have lived in comfort; and we spend vast sums of money arming for war. So just how civilized are we? If we succeed in building a fairer and more peaceful world in the future, we may look back and find that 20th-century humanity was not very civilized after all.

The traditions of ancient civilizations live on today. Here crowds assemble for the Q'Collor-Riti festival in the Peruvian Andes, honouring the snow-capped mountain Auzangate. This is one of several peaks believed to have been the protectors of Cuzco, the capital of the ancient Inca empire.

INTRODUCTION

CIVILIZATION

LIVING IN CITIES

Bright lights, big city! Cities can be exciting places, with their busy streets, crowded markets, inviting shops, cinemas and theatres, interesting museums, and much more. Many people think that cities represent what modern life is all about. Some people love them, and others say they hate them. How important are cities in our world today?

Dhaka, capital city of Bangladesh, has severe traffic congestion in the rush-hour, like big cities everywhere. Many people use cycle rickshaws to get around: they are cheap and reliable, and do not pollute the environment.

The first civilizations had small settlements of only a few thousand people. In the Middle Ages the world's larger cities had 40,000 or more inhabitants. By the mid-1800s several cities, including London, Paris, New York, Tokyo, and Shanghai, had populations of more than one million. Today's largest cities, such as Mexico City and Tokyo-Yokohama, have more than 20 million inhabitants.

What cities have to offer

The inhabitants of cities have achieved great things. The Roman Empire, for example, with its architecture, engineering, law, literature, and system of government, was completely city-based. Cities today offer many of the facilities of modern life that people enjoy, from opera houses and art galleries to pop music and fashion.

Yet almost from the beginning cities have had problems – poverty, overcrowding, crime, disease, and pollution. Large cities need huge supplies of food and could not survive without the surrounding countryside. They make huge demands on energy supplies, **raw materials**, and cheap human labour for their industries.

Many cities in developed countries have stopped growing as people move away from them, seeking more pleasant surroundings in the **suburbs** and semi-rural areas. In contrast, far greater numbers of people in developing countries who want to escape from poverty leave the countryside and move to cities. By the year 2000 more than half the human race will live in cities, compared with only 14 per cent in 1900.

Main airline routes linking cities

Cities are centres of knowledge, ideas, and information. They are home to most large libraries, newspaper and book publishing, and television and radio broadcasting.

Money was once mainly just a tool of trade. Now money itself is traded. New York, Frankfurt, Tokyo, and other cities are powerful banking and finance centres whose decisions can affect the lives of millions of people worldwide.

Architecture – the design and construction of buildings – is an important urban art form. The ruins of many fine monuments show the glories of past city-based civilizations.

3000 BC

200 BC

CITIES AND CIVILIZATION
Every civilization has involved people living in cities. The link between cities and civilization is just as strong today. Cities can be places of opportunity, wealth creation, culture, and new ideas. But they could not exist without a network of support links providing energy, food, and communications.

26

RESOURCES

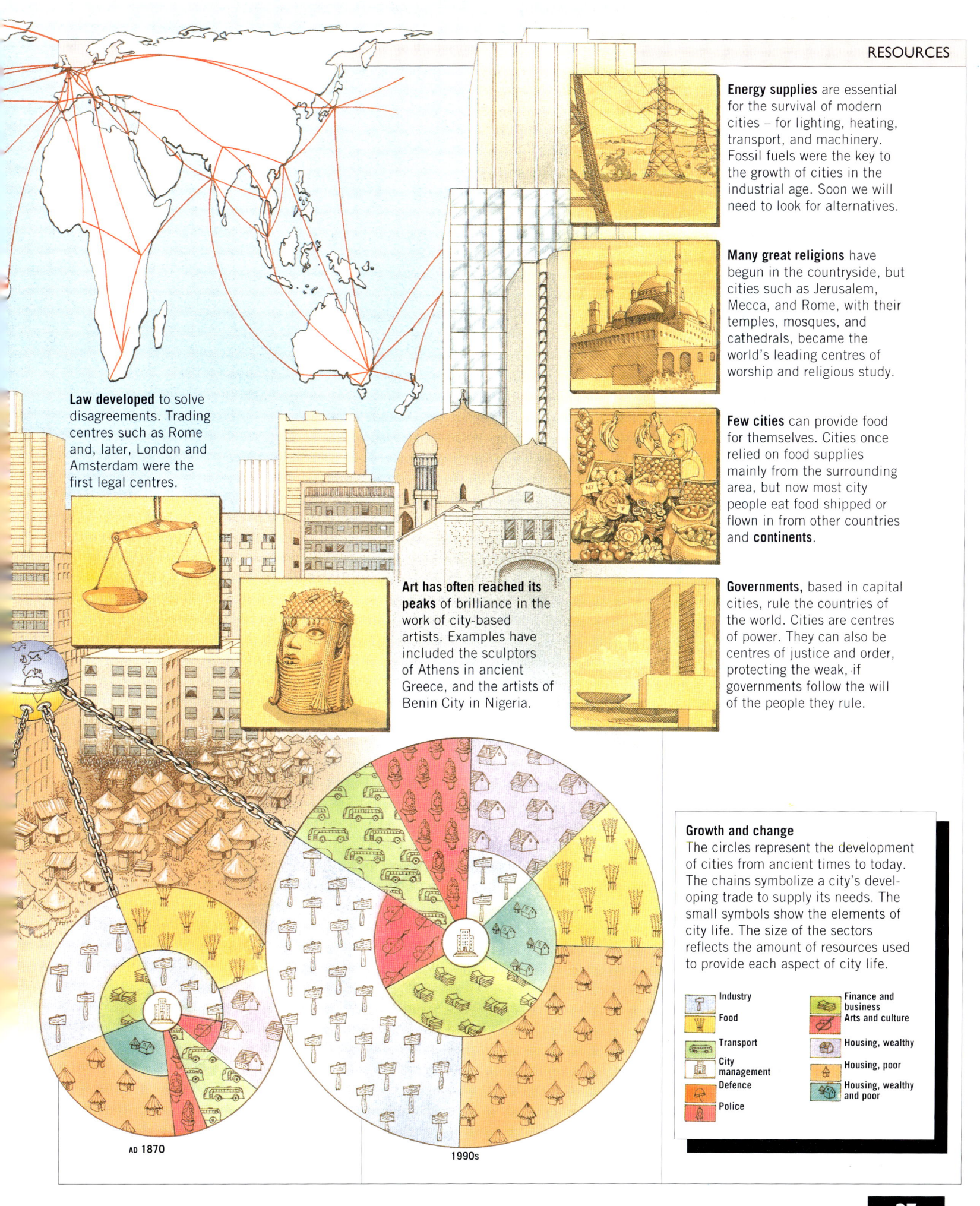

Energy supplies are essential for the survival of modern cities – for lighting, heating, transport, and machinery. Fossil fuels were the key to the growth of cities in the industrial age. Soon we will need to look for alternatives.

Many great religions have begun in the countryside, but cities such as Jerusalem, Mecca, and Rome, with their temples, mosques, and cathedrals, became the world's leading centres of worship and religious study.

Few cities can provide food for themselves. Cities once relied on food supplies mainly from the surrounding area, but now most city people eat food shipped or flown in from other countries and **continents**.

Governments, based in capital cities, rule the countries of the world. Cities are centres of power. They can also be centres of justice and order, protecting the weak, if governments follow the will of the people they rule.

Law developed to solve disagreements. Trading centres such as Rome and, later, London and Amsterdam were the first legal centres.

Art has often reached its peaks of brilliance in the work of city-based artists. Examples have included the sculptors of Athens in ancient Greece, and the artists of Benin City in Nigeria.

Growth and change
The circles represent the development of cities from ancient times to today. The chains symbolize a city's developing trade to supply its needs. The small symbols show the elements of city life. The size of the sectors reflects the amount of resources used to provide each aspect of city life.

- Industry
- Food
- Transport
- City management
- Defence
- Police
- Finance and business
- Arts and culture
- Housing, wealthy
- Housing, poor
- Housing, wealthy and poor

AD 1870

1990s

27

CIVILIZATION

WORLD FACTORY

Are you good at making things? You may be a clever model-maker, or skilful with a needle and thread or electrical circuits. It is natural to enjoy making things well, and sometimes our skills can earn money for us. But problems may develop if making goods and selling them become more important to us than anything else.

Before the Industrial Revolution began in the 18th century, people made furniture, clothes, and other goods on a small scale. They used mainly water power, animal power, and their own hands. Trade was mainly local. Modern industry developed as people began to burn coal to produce steam to power machines making more and more goods in factories.

Britain, France, Spain, Portugal, and the Netherlands had grown rich through conquest and slavery. They controlled much of Africa, Asia, the Caribbean, and Central and South America, and sent millions of Africans to work as slaves in the Americas. Britain led the world in making and trading goods around the world. Germany, the USA, and other countries followed on the road to industrialization. Countries such as Brazil are developing their industries in the same way today.

The inventions and new technologies of the 19th and 20th centuries – from electricity and conveyor belts to information technology (IT) and **biotechnology** – have transformed world industry.

In the Americas industry's share of wealth creation is between 30% and 40%. The USA leads the world in manufacturing.

Industry, employment, and wealth
The importance of industry in creating wealth varies from region to region, as does the number of people working in services (shops, banks, offices, and so on) as opposed to farming. Industrial development depends on industrial research, and the amount of money spent on it. The money value of manufacturing (making goods from raw materials) reveals the importance of industry to a country's economy.

DID YOU KNOW?

The biggest businesses
Huge global companies called **multinationals** control about a third of the world's major industries and employ millions of people. Their activities include mining and oil production, farming, scientific research, **manufacturing**, advertising, and marketing. The largest **corporations**, such as General Motors in the USA, are richer than many countries.

Manufacturing industry
Manufacturing – the large-scale production of finished goods from raw materials – is the main activity of modern industry. A constant flow of industrial products (such as chemicals, steel, and machinery) and consumer goods (such as cars, household items, and clothes) comes from the world's factories. Can we make manufacturing less environmentally damaging?

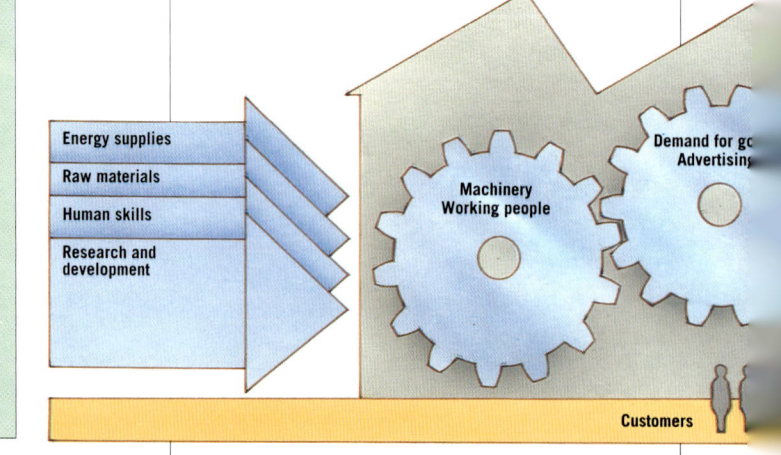

In Africa industry's share of wealth creation is only 25%. In the Middle East the share is a massive 60%, including oil production.

Germany and Japan come second to the USA among industrial countries, judged by the size of their manufacturing economies.

Industry's share of wealth creation, shown by height of region	Employment	Research and development scientists and engineers in region	Twelve leading industrial countries
70% 60% 50% 40% 30% 20% 10%	More jobs in services than in farming / More jobs in farming than in services / Value added in manufacturing 1990 / $200,000 million / $50,000 million	500 for every 1 million people / Less than 500 for every 1 million people	1 Canada 7 Germany 2 USA 8 France 3 Mexico 9 Spain 4 Brazil 10 Italy 5 UK 11 Israel 6 Belgium 12 Japan

Research and development
We invest large amounts of money researching and developing new products and technologies. A quarter of this money is for weapons research. Developed countries spend the most on research and development; developing countries have little money available.

Share of research and development spending in 1990
World total $175,000 million

- North America 41%
- Europe 41%
- Asia 14%
- Africa 0.5%
- Middle East 0.5%
- Oceania 1%
- Latin America 2%

Manufacturing industry has been the key to wealth creation in developed countries, along with trade. Developing countries know that it can help them too. More and more factories may create wealth, but not necessarily a better quality of life.

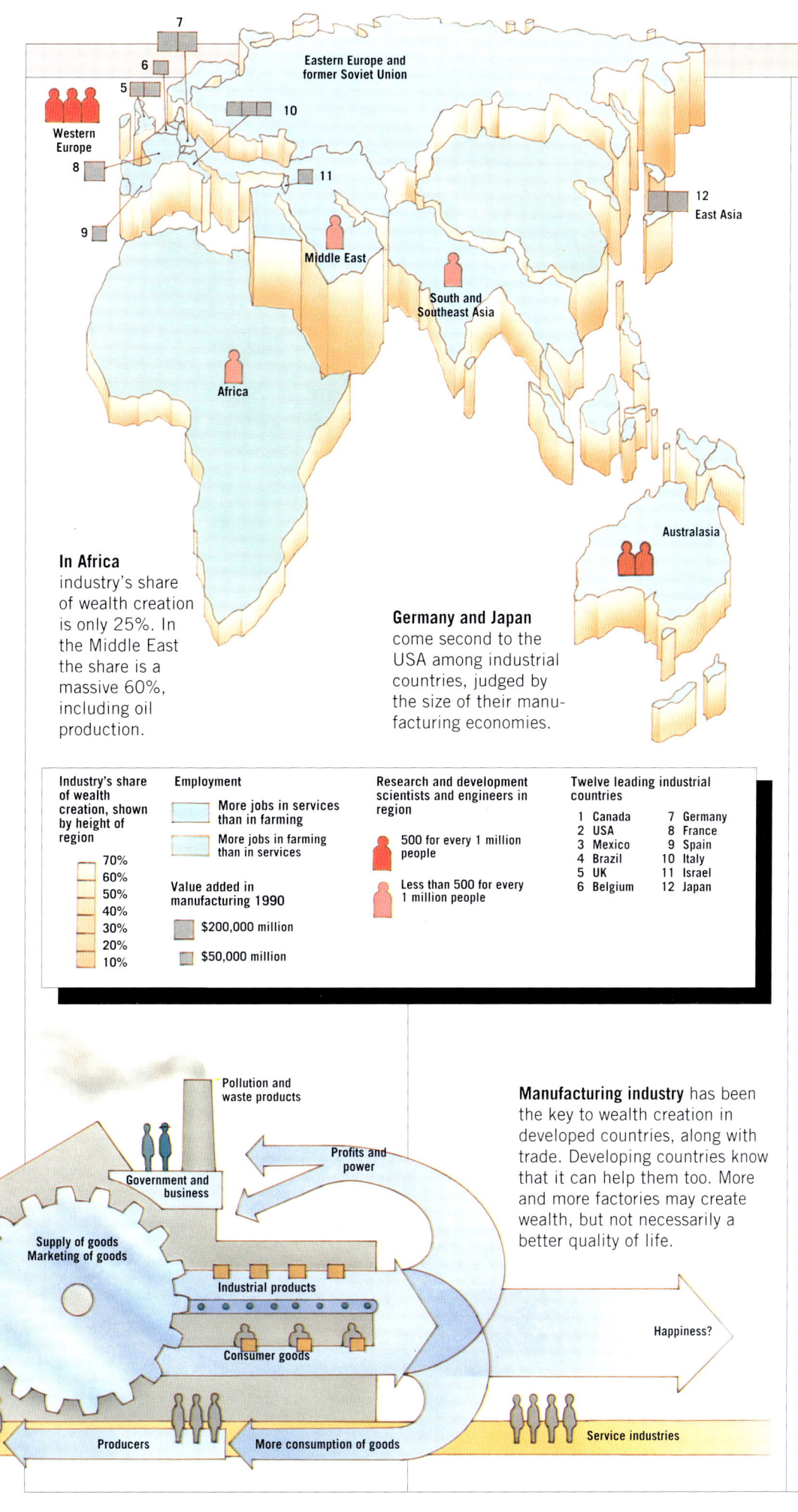

The price of industrialization
Industry and world trade have brought many benefits to human-kind. More people than ever have long, comfortable, and interesting lives, and enjoy goods and services unknown to their ancestors. Yet some people question whether the disadvantages of an industrialized world outweigh the advantages.

Much of the wealth that we "create" comes from using up non-**renewable** resources, such as oil and **minerals**. Large-scale, modern industry can harm traditional communities and cause widespread environmental damage. The world's weapons armoury has continued to grow through the **arms trade**. And although we now have many brilliant medical treatments, millions of men, women, and children still die from a lack of food and clean water.

The wealth gap between rich and poor has widened within countries and between the developed and developing worlds. If all countries produced and consumed in the way the developed world does today, our environment would soon become a wasteland.

29

CIVILIZATION

COMMUNICATION

Communication means sending and receiving information, ideas, thoughts, and feelings. Many people today have a wide choice of communication technologies at their fingertips: newspapers and magazines, books, the telephone, radio, television, and computers. Computer and satellite communications have developed enormously in the last 20 years. We can now store all the material from a book such as this on a tiny **microchip** and send information across the world in seconds.

Modern communications can help solve problems. In developing countries, radio is a good way to communicate information about preventing disease and improving health, and about family planning practices. It is especially useful where many people do not read.

Speech and language are the basis of most human communication. Nearly all the world's languages belong to a small number of language groups. As early people increased in number and spread around the world, languages in the same group became different from each other. The first human writing may be cave-wall "picture stories" from about 30,000 BC. By 3300 BC people in the Middle East used a form of **cuneiform**, or word-picture writing, that is probably the long distant ancestor of the Latin alphabet.

Computers are probably the most important and fastest-changing communications and information technology today. Early machines were large and expensive. Hundreds of millions of people and businesses now use cheaper, desktop computers.

Like many young people, you probably spend a lot of time at a computer keyboard. You belong to one of the first "computer generations". Most people growing up 15 or 20 years ago did not have computer rooms at school or college, or a word processor at home. Even today, hundreds of millions of people in some parts of the world will never use a computer – or even a telephone.

FROM THE BIRTH OF LANGUAGE TO THE INTERNET
Speech was the first human system of communication. Over time people have invented a whole series of new ways to send and receive information and messages: long-distance signals and sounds, printing, the telegraph and telephone, radio and television, satellite technology, and computer networks. Each new technology has been a step in the transformation of communications. Today's Internet gives a person seated at a computer speedy access to an almost limitless range of other people, discussion groups, and information sources all over the world. "Interactive" programs and technologies promise a wide variety of future developments.

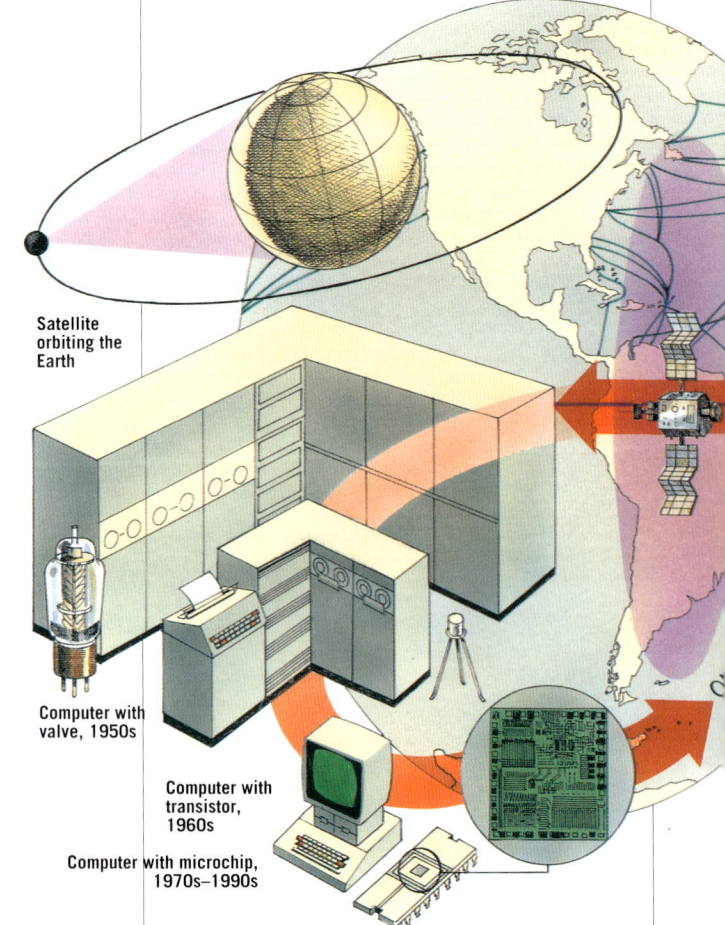

Satellite orbiting the Earth

Computer with valve, 1950s

Computer with transistor, 1960s

Computer with microchip, 1970s–1990s

RESOURCES

Early systems of sending long-distance messages included drum beats (a method still used in parts of Africa), beacon fires, flags, and knotted ropes.

The first printers used carved stone and wooden blocks. Printing using wooden movable type began in China and northern Europe in the 15th century.

The telegraph and telephone, in the 19th century, were the first electrical forms of long-distance communication. Telephones now use satellite links.

"Wireless" radio followed soon after Marconi had invented the wireless telegraph in 1895. The first regular radio broadcasts, by the BBC, began in 1922.

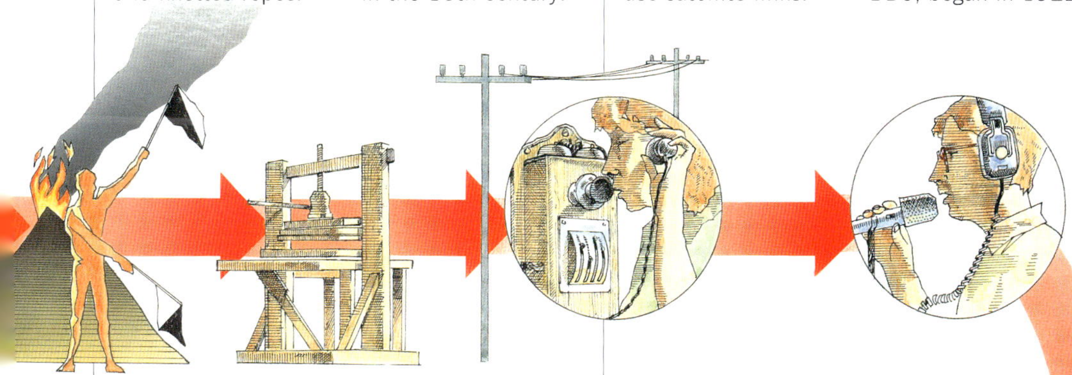

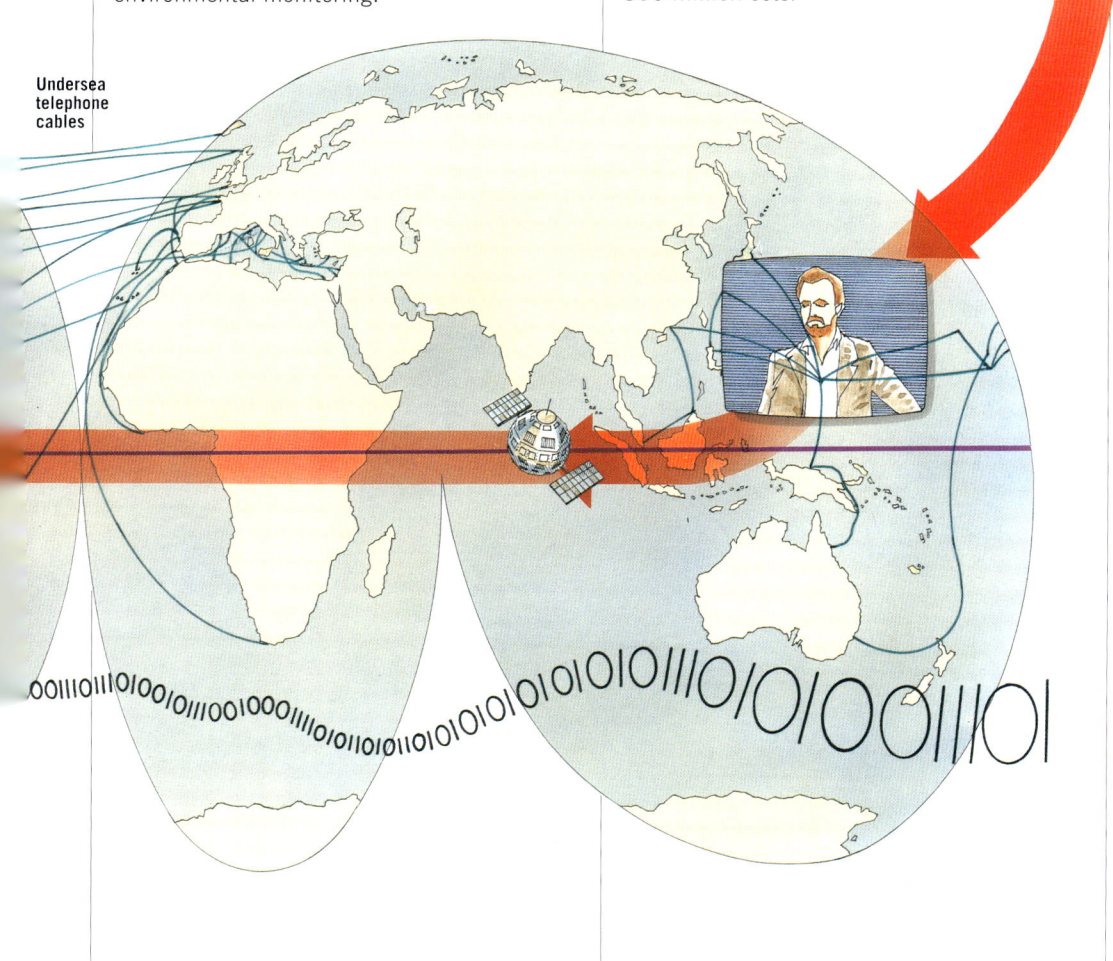

With satellite technology we can map the Earth's surface and see what is happening to forests, farmland, lakes, rivers, and seas.

Yet not everyone benefits equally from modern communications networks. Less than one person in a hundred in developing countries has a television set. A few giant corporations own many newspapers and television and computer companies. These corporations, and some governments, have great control over the information we receive. People watch US-made television programmes and films, for example, all over the world.

Another worry is that governments and businesses can use computers secretly to gather, store, and exchange private information about people.

Thousands of satellites have gone into orbit since the first launch in 1957, but only a few hundred remain circling the Earth. We use them mainly for television and telephone links, weather forecasting, and geological and environmental monitoring.

Television was invented in the 1920s, and the first regular broadcasts began ten years later. TV is now one of our most powerful forms of communication. People in developed countries own well over half the world's 850 million sets.

Remote sensing by satellite reveals information about the Earth that is much harder to see on the ground. Different rocks reflect sunlight differently. Pictures taken by satellite are colour-coded on computer to show these differences, as here. Identifying rocks may reveal mineral deposits.

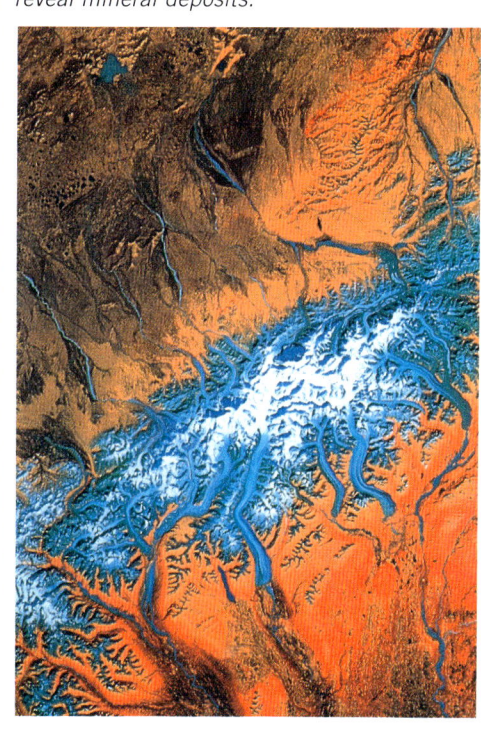

Undersea telephone cables

31

CIVILIZATION

CHAOS IN THE CITY

About 2400 million people live in cities today. This is four times as many as 45 years ago. City populations are growing particularly fast in developing countries. In these countries almost half the city population increase results from people moving in from the countryside – at a rate of 75,000 each day worldwide.

The growing urban population
By the end of the 20th century, for the first time, half the world's people will live in urban areas (towns and cities). The proportion will rise to 60 per cent by 2020, leaving just two out of every five people in the countryside.

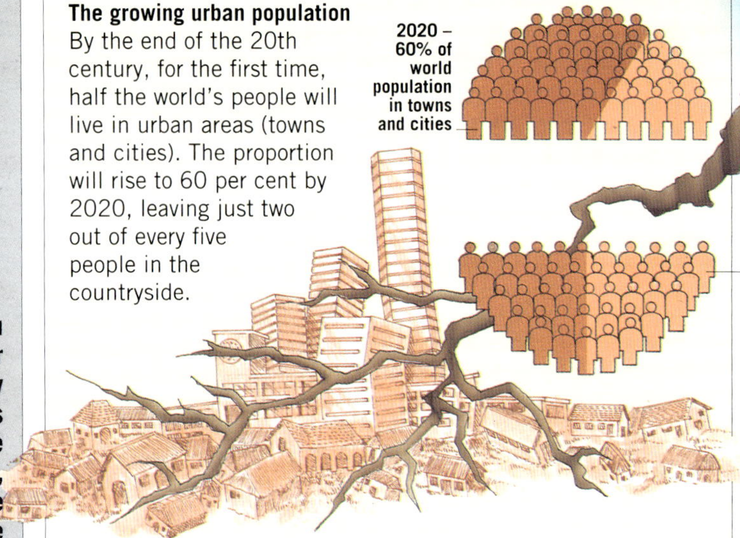

2020 – 60% of world population in towns and cities

2000 – 50% of world population in towns and cities

Is there a neighbourhood near where you live that you try to avoid, especially after dark? Most of us know such places. They are badly lit, dirty, ugly, and trouble seems to lurk in the shadows. You may find these areas unpleasant enough to walk through, but for the people living there, they are even worse. Many cities have large areas like this, and they present many problems worldwide.

Why do so many people migrate to the cities in developing countries? As large-scale farming, **forestry**, and other forms of development increase, natural resources, including land, become scarcer. Poor people who once earned a living off the land find it harder to survive. So they head for the cities looking for work.

Most newcomers join many other poor city dwellers in **shanty towns** fringing the suburbs and business districts. Usually shelter is in shacks built from scrap metal, plastic, and cardboard. There is often no piped water, electricity, sanitation, or refuse disposal.

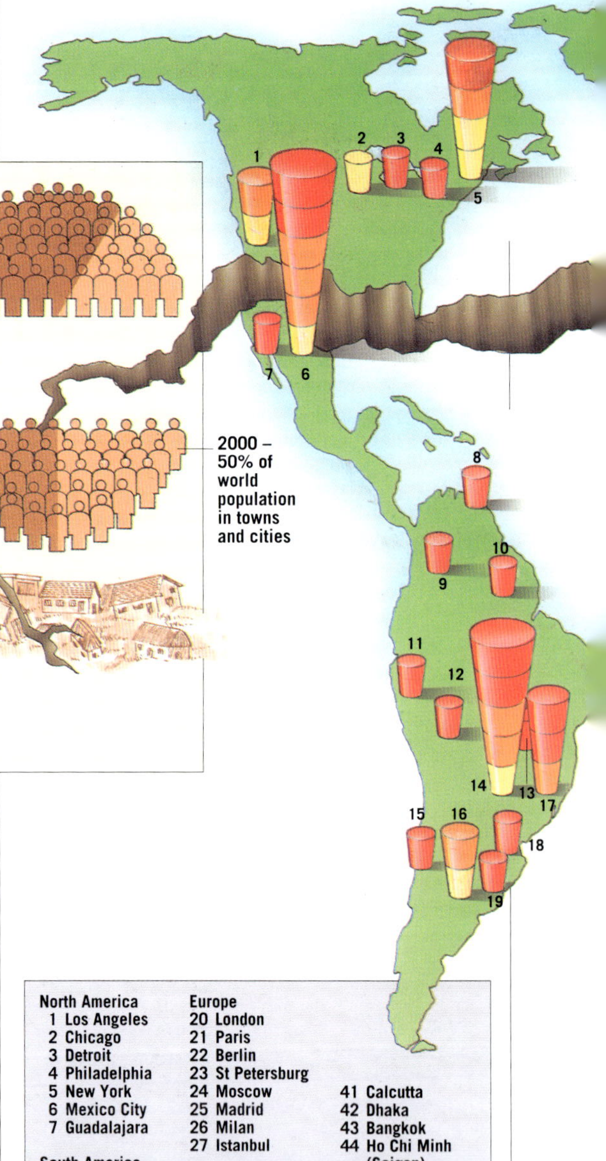

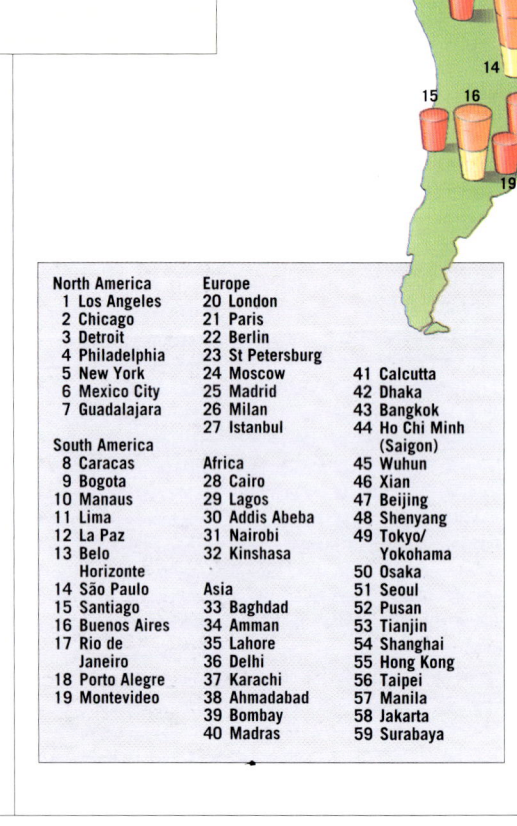

DID YOU KNOW?

Choked-up cities
Many millions of people in cities have poor health because of heavy road traffic near their homes. Children, pregnant women, and older people living near main roads suffer more than most. Noise and danger from traffic disturb neighbourhoods and cut people off from each other. In London, Europe's most expensive capital city for public transport, car traffic moves at an average speed of 15 km (8 miles) an hour – as slowly as a horse and cart! Many cities in Western Europe and elsewhere are finding ways to reduce traffic congestion and pollution.

North America
1 Los Angeles
2 Chicago
3 Detroit
4 Philadelphia
5 New York
6 Mexico City
7 Guadalajara

South America
8 Caracas
9 Bogota
10 Manaus
11 Lima
12 La Paz
13 Belo Horizonte
14 São Paulo
15 Santiago
16 Buenos Aires
17 Rio de Janeiro
18 Porto Alegre
19 Montevideo

Europe
20 London
21 Paris
22 Berlin
23 St Petersburg
24 Moscow
25 Madrid
26 Milan
27 Istanbul

Africa
28 Cairo
29 Lagos
30 Addis Abeba
31 Nairobi
32 Kinshasa

Asia
33 Baghdad
34 Amman
35 Lahore
36 Delhi
37 Karachi
38 Ahmadabad
39 Bombay
40 Madras
41 Calcutta
42 Dhaka
43 Bangkok
44 Ho Chi Minh (Saigon)
45 Wuhun
46 Xian
47 Beijing
48 Shenyang
49 Tokyo/Yokohama
50 Osaka
51 Seoul
52 Pusan
53 Tianjin
54 Shanghai
55 Hong Kong
56 Taipei
57 Manila
58 Jakarta
59 Surabaya

PROBLEMS

GROWTH OF THE WORLD'S CITIES

In 1950 only seven of the world's cities had a population of more than five million. By 1990, ten cities contained more than ten million people. By the year 2010 there could be 60 cities of around five million inhabitants, and several giant cities of between 15 million and 20 million people. The map shows that almost all the world's fast-growing cities are in developing countries, to the south of the **North-South** divide. Mexico City could become the first city of 30 million inhabitants.

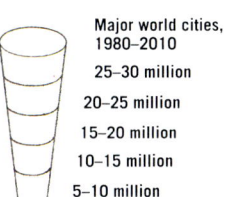

Major world cities, 1980–2010
- 25–30 million
- 20–25 million
- 15–20 million
- 10–15 million
- 5–10 million
- Up to 5 million

- Population growth to 2010
- Population in 1995
- Population in 1980

Life in a shanty town

Hunger, overcrowding, pollution, and sickness are common in shanty towns. So is underemployment. Many children have no schooling, and many families do not have access to health services. To survive and raise children in these terrible surroundings is a great struggle.

The governments of developing countries do not always do enough to help people in shanty towns. They may spend more money on motorways, airports, and business districts than on helping the poor improve their living conditions. People in poor neighbourhoods may be treated like criminals by the police, especially if they are squatting on land belonging to others. When a city council wants to sell or build on land where there is a shanty town, the shacks get bulldozed to the ground.

Cities of the developed world

Cities in developed countries also have problems, although on a smaller scale. Many industries and businesses have shut down or moved out of town, often leaving derelict buildings behind. Higher-earning people have moved to the suburbs, where pleasant shops, schools, workplaces, and other facilities are a car drive away. Inner-city services such as community housing, public transport, libraries, and parks are underfunded and neglected. Many once-prosperous city centres are now unpleasant, unsafe, and troubled by vandalism and crime.

The tumbledown houses of a shanty town in Kennedy Town, west Hong Kong, cling precariously to a steep slope.

CIVILIZATION

HAVES & HAVE-NOTS

It is natural to enjoy spending money. Hardly anybody could live without it at all. Yet, because it is important to so many, money can have undesirable effects. It can turn friends into enemies. It also "breeds": those who have a lot of it seem to get more. Money means power in many places, and it has a great impact on our world.

HOME ACTION

It will take many generations to end poverty, but we can all play a part.
- Try to live more simply and spend less money on yourself.
- Where possible, buy fair-traded goods, which provide higher incomes for producers (at slightly higher cost to the customer).
- Give unwanted clothes, gifts, and so on to a local charity shop.
- Support, or work as a volunteer for, an anti-poverty group.
- When you have money to save, use an "ethnical" bank or savings scheme; that is, one that avoids making unfair profits from developing countries.
- Find out more about living conditions in poor countries and help spread the word.

The wealth gap between the rich, developed countries of the North (including Australia and New Zealand) and the poor, developing countries of the South is wide and growing wider. People in North America, Western Europe, and Japan are about 60 times richer, on average, than those in developing countries. With just 20 per cent of the world's people, the North has 75 per cent of its income.

How the rich got rich

What has produced the wealth gap? Many countries in the North once had empires and colonies in the South, and grew rich partly at their expense. They built up their industries at home using cheap raw materials from the countries they ruled. They sold goods, such as machinery and processed foods, to less developed countries for big profits. (Of course, some people stayed quite poor in the richer, industrial countries.) Rising profits and high consumption levels in the North have meant ever larger **debts** in the South and have damaged environments worldwide.

A few developing countries, such as Brazil, South Korea, and India, have become wealthier by developing industry. But most of the developing world can never take this route. There are not enough raw materials, and the environment could not cope with the pollution. In many countries of Africa, most people are no better off than they were 30 years ago.

Within developing countries too, there is a gap between rich and poor. A few politicians, business people, and others live in comfort, but many are trapped in poverty.

THE POVERTY BOMB

More than 1000 million people worldwide live in total poverty. They lack decent living conditions, enough food, education, paid work, access to health or transport services and, in most cases, government help. As the map shows, all except a few of the very poorest people live in the developing countries of the South. Widespread severe poverty can have devastating effects – like a bomb exploding – leading to massive outbreaks of disease, environmental damage, and violent rioting.

Percentage of a country's people living in worst poverty, 1990
- More than 65%
- 45–65%
- 25–44%
- 5–24%
- Less than 5%
- No information
- Poorest countries: less than $500 of wealth created per person per year

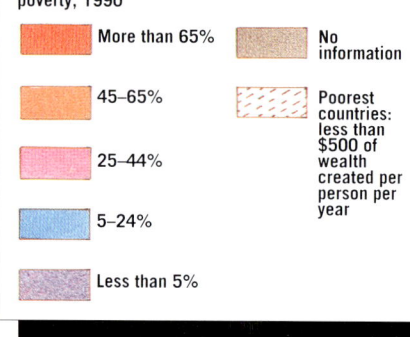

Aid and trade

In 1990 Northern banks and governments gave or lent the South $5600 million. Many loans depend on the involvement of Northern businesses. In 1990 Northern companies made profits of more than $13,000 million from working in the South. Aid from development charities usually works better.

PROBLEMS

The debt crisis
Developing countries owe many millions of dollars to banks in developed countries. For decades, the prices of their goods have fallen while the costs of imports have risen. They have borrowed more and more money to keep going, especially in the 1970s and early 1980s. Much money was spent on big projects, such as power stations. Banks were less interested in lending money to improve health, housing, or literacy. Few countries have paid off the loans. High interest rates (the cost of borrowing), have meant that most now owe more than they borrowed in the first place.

At the Earth Summit in Rio de Janeiro, Brazil, in 1992, many developed countries agreed under the Biodiversity Convention to provide financial and technical support to help developing countries protect their wild areas. In return, the developed world gained access to biological resources such as rainforest plant species. Here Al Gore, later to become US Vice-President, speaks at the Summit.

35

CIVILIZATION

WORLD AT WAR

Are you an aggressive person? Most likely not. You would probably try very hard to avoid becoming involved in a violent situation. Most people feel the same. Yet there has hardly been a time when the whole world was at peace, and it is far from peaceful today. Many people worry that environmental problems will lead to conflict, unless we solve them first.

Since 1945 there have been at least 170 wars. Most have taken place in developing countries, using weapons sold by developed countries. Twenty-two million people have died in these wars, and millions more have been injured or become refugees. Some thinkers argue that most wars are fought over land, raw materials, and wealth, and not because human beings are naturally aggressive.

The end of the **Cold War** between the West and the Soviet Union brought the promise of peace. But it was followed by new wars, such as that in the former Yugoslavia. Many wars are "civil wars" between different groups of people in the same country. **Civil wars** often begin when some people have too much power over others, or because of struggles over resources such as land.

Soldiers have always died in war, but modern war kills more **civilians** (non-fighting citizens) than soldiers. During the 1980s, for example, 85 per cent of people who died in war were civilians.

Each year the world spends a massive $1,000,000 million on weapons and war. The price of a nuclear submarine would pay to educate children in 23 developing countries for a year. For the cost of a day's fighting in the 1991 Gulf War we could have saved five million children's lives through health programmes. Two days' worth of world "defence" spending would enable us to tackle the spread of deserts. Five hours' worth would fund the UN's Environment Programme for up to ten years, and seven months' worth would pay for Agenda 21, the UN action plan for sustainable development.

Casualties of war
Between 1945 and 1995 nearly 22 million people died in wars, most of them civilians.

Region	Civilians killed	Soldiers killed
Europe	290,000	70,000
South Asia	2,200,000	1,100,000
Far East	6,600,000	4,100,000
Middle East	440,000	600,000
Latin America	460,000	200,000
Africa	3,800,000	1,700,000
Total	13,790,000	7,770,000

36

PROBLEMS

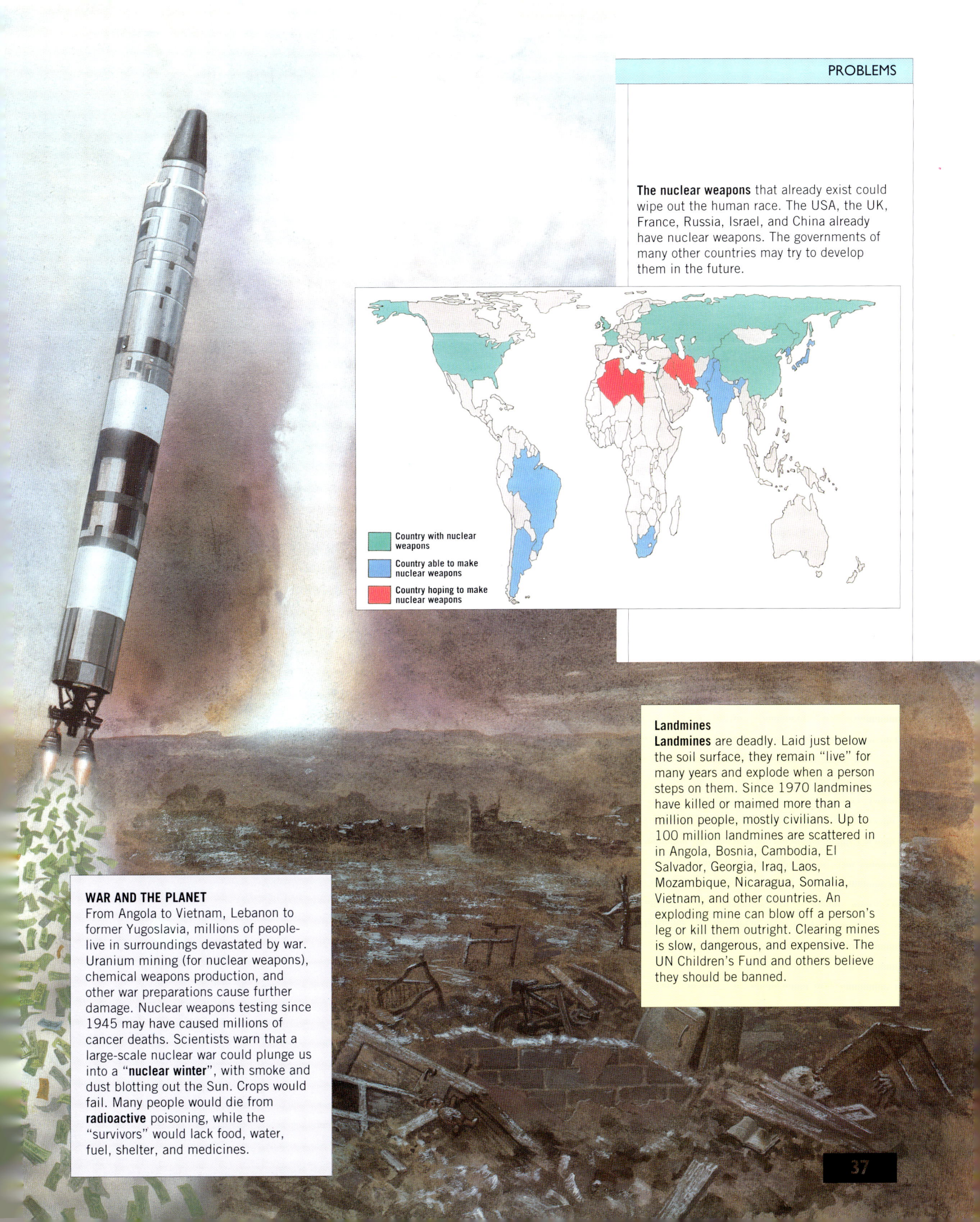

The nuclear weapons that already exist could wipe out the human race. The USA, the UK, France, Russia, Israel, and China already have nuclear weapons. The governments of many other countries may try to develop them in the future.

- Country with nuclear weapons
- Country able to make nuclear weapons
- Country hoping to make nuclear weapons

Landmines
Landmines are deadly. Laid just below the soil surface, they remain "live" for many years and explode when a person steps on them. Since 1970 landmines have killed or maimed more than a million people, mostly civilians. Up to 100 million landmines are scattered in in Angola, Bosnia, Cambodia, El Salvador, Georgia, Iraq, Laos, Mozambique, Nicaragua, Somalia, Vietnam, and other countries. An exploding mine can blow off a person's leg or kill them outright. Clearing mines is slow, dangerous, and expensive. The UN Children's Fund and others believe they should be banned.

WAR AND THE PLANET
From Angola to Vietnam, Lebanon to former Yugoslavia, millions of people live in surroundings devastated by war. Uranium mining (for nuclear weapons), chemical weapons production, and other war preparations cause further damage. Nuclear weapons testing since 1945 may have caused millions of cancer deaths. Scientists warn that a large-scale nuclear war could plunge us into a **"nuclear winter"**, with smoke and dust blotting out the Sun. Crops would fail. Many people would die from **radioactive** poisoning, while the "survivors" would lack food, water, fuel, shelter, and medicines.

GAIA WATCH

COMMUNITY GROUPS

"We are so far from anywhere that the government doesn't even know that animals live here," says Yaqub Baloch.

"Here" is Kharochan, about as far south as you can go in Pakistan before ending up in the Rann of Kutch, an area of salt and mud-flats on the border of India and Pakistan. It is hot: the land is flat and barren, with a few acacias and thorn scrub. It is hard to imagine anyone making a living here. There are few roads, schools, or clinics. People survive by growing bananas and vegetables.

In 1992 Yaqub Baloch and his friends had an idea: "We heard on

▲ **In Kharochan** (main picture), villagers are working together to make life easier in a harsh region that has scorching temperatures and sparse vegetation, and is subject to sudden floods in the rainy season. Teams of people dig drainage channels or build walls of earth to protect the roads.

◄ **Villagers are trying** to protect their homes from flooding. Soil is piled up around the houses, and in the courtyards, and packed down to make a firm base, higher than the surrounding land.

► **Kharochan is so hot** that houses are built to allow as much air as possible to blow through the walls and keep them cool. The houses are often flooded during the monsoon, so everyone keeps most of their belongings off the ground.

the radio, and read in the newspapers, that there are village organizations working for change and improving life for people in their villages.

"We called a meeting of some friends, and put forward the idea that we should form such a group. There was a lot of debate, but finally 12 of us decided to form the *tanzeem* (community group). The first thing we did was to rebuild a section of road destroyed by floods.

"Then some friends told us that Oxfam might help us. So, after the floods in 1994, we wrote to them. Because of the emergency situation they provided money to buy food for 400 of the most needy people." The *tanzeem* worked to raise houses above flood level and build better flood defences.

The community group has demonstrated that working together can get results. Its efforts provided food and jobs when both were in short supply. Yaqub says: "Now people have seen that there is a point to the *tanzeem*, and they are showing their support. If we work hard for ourselves, others may see our struggle and join hands with us."

◄ **People need to be able to move safely** from village to village during the monsoon season, or whenever there is flooding, so the roads are being raised above the highest flood level. The villagers work together in shifts, day and night, so that the work will get finished sooner.

CIVILIZATION

ACTION FOR CITIES

People are already putting good ideas into practice to solve city problems. The aim is to make cities healthier, safer, "greener", and more people-friendly. City neighbourhoods in both developed and developing countries need adequate, affordable housing; local shops, services, and markets; well-maintained schools and community centres; small-scale workplaces and local businesses; parks and other open spaces; and safe, pleasant roads.

In developed countries a partnership between local and central government, community groups, and private businesses provides the best mix of skills and resources. In developing countries neighbourhood improvement schemes need government funding and technical advice but should rely on the skills of local people.

CITY ACTION IN DEVELOPING COUNTRIES
Developing countries can involve local people in low-cost schemes to improve poor neighbourhoods. Given tools, technical help, loans, basic services, and legal rights to land, shanty-town dwellers prove to be excellent neighbourhood builders and managers.

Improving a shanty town
1. Laying water and sewage pipes.
2. Link-up to electricity supplies.
3. Locally run refuse collection.
4. Local people build houses, helped by government and development groups.
5. Community centre and planning office, run by local people.
6. Old shanty-town area.
7. Street lights and trees.
8. New market area with water well.

Imagine a perfect city. What would it be like? In some ways it might be similar to the city you live in or one you know. But the chances are that you would want more parks and open spaces, cleaner streets, safer roads, an end to city poverty, and more friendly neighbourhoods. It is possible to redesign our city surroundings for real.

DID YOU KNOW?

Poor people take the lead
People in shanty towns in Latin America have a talent for getting organized. In 1985 an earthquake in Mexico City wrecked hundreds of homes in one poor neighbourhood. Landlords wanted to redevelop the area. But local people, led mainly by women, set up a rebuilding programme that the city council paid for. Homeless people in Lima, Peru, and in Buenos Aires, Argentina, have "invaded" unused land, and built homes, roads, schools, and community centres, organized rubbish clearance, planted trees, and started food co-operatives.

SOLUTIONS

Many poor city dwellers live in temporary homes with no services on unused or waste land. In Recife, in Brazil, an organization helps people to get the legal rights to the land they are living on. It then helps them build permanent homes to replace the temporary ones, as here, and get services such as water, sanitation, and electricity.

Making big cities better

Easing the burden on cities in developing countries depends on improving living conditions in the countryside and small towns, thus reducing country-to-city migration.

Many governments spend far more money encouraging big business than they do on inner-city or shanty-town renewal. This is because they think that wealth from big business will "trickle down" to help the poor. In the UK, the government has invested huge sums in London's Docklands. Yet this major new business district is close to some of the worst inner-city conditions in Western Europe. Developing countries too are often more interested in helping foreign companies build factories than in improving slum housing.

Governments need a fairer and "greener" approach to the creation of wealth. This means more spending on basic health services, welfare, and education; less special treatment for big business; tighter pollution controls; higher taxes on environmentally harmful products and activities; the promotion of energy efficiency and recycling; a switch to more environment-friendly forms of transport; more support for community groups; and better local democracy, so people can make decisions about their own neighbourhoods.

CITY ACTION IN DEVELOPED COUNTRIES
Local communities have a say in the most succesful inner-city renewal schemes. These projects improve old buildings, encourage "self-build" housing communities, provide green spaces, create workshops, and promote environment-friendly forms of transport.

Renewing the inner city
1. New community centre and nursery.
2. New energy-efficient housing.
3. Old houses upgraded.
4. Street improvements: road humps, trees, and landscaping.
5. Wall painting by local artist and children.
6. Neighbourhood planning office and shops.
7. New park and playground.
8. New workshops and offices.
9. New local bus route.

41

CIVILIZATION

CLOSING THE GAP

What makes some countries, and some people, poor? There are those who say it is their own fault for not trying hard enough. Others argue that poverty just can't be helped. This chapter has tried to show that wealth and poverty are part of the same problem – injustice. If we could all agree on that, we would be halfway to doing something about it.

Joint efforts between people from North and South on development projects can be very successful. Here in West Africa, a US wildlife agency, the Sierra Leone Ministry of Agriculture, and researchers from US and African universities come together to help the local people build a wildlife sanctuary and research station.

The fates of developed and developing countries are closely connected. High living standards in the North depend on the supply of raw materials from the South. Northern industries need Southern customers. Both "halves" of the world need each other to help protect the planet from environmental damage. But besides all this, can people in developed countries be happy knowing that millions of their fellow human beings are struggling in poverty?

Trade, aid, and development can help us close the wealth gap between developed and developing countries. But perhaps we need to change our idea of trade. More is not always better. Fairer and more

One year's wealth creation (1991)
- Poorest countries: average wealth creation $350 per person
- Middle-income countries: average wealth creation $2000 per person
- Richest countries: average wealth creation $14,900 per person

Aid from international organizations, 1960–90
- $50,000 million
- $40,000 million
- $30,000 million
- $20,000 million
- $10,000 million
- $0

Aid-giving as a share of developed countries' wealth creation, 1990
- 1.6%
- 1.2%
- 0.8%
- 0.4%

Developed countries' wealth creation per person, 1991: $14,900

North-South income gap, 1991: $14,020 per person

Developing countries wealth creation per person, 1991: $880

World trade links countries together. Developing countries that remain very poor do not make good trading partners. Long-lasting trade depends on both sides getting fair prices for their goods. More trade between developing countries themselves, and less reliance on developed countries, could help them overcome their poverty.

SOLUTIONS

sensible trade would mean that countries where people go hungry never had to grow luxury foods to sell abroad, rather than food to feed their own people. And there would be fairer shares of trading profits.

Many people believe that aid to developing countries should also change. Too much money has been wasted on large-scale projects that fail to improve the lives of ordinary people. Aid has often made the rich richer and the poor poorer. We are learning to target aid money more carefully, so that the poorest people benefit most.

Both trade and aid can help pay for development. Yet forms of development that look impressive are not always effective. What use to a poor country are motorways, for example, if millions of its people cannot even afford a bicycle?

World leaders have met at many conferences to discuss ways of bridging the gap between rich North and poor South. A wide range of solutions are possible. Working together, we can win the war against poverty.

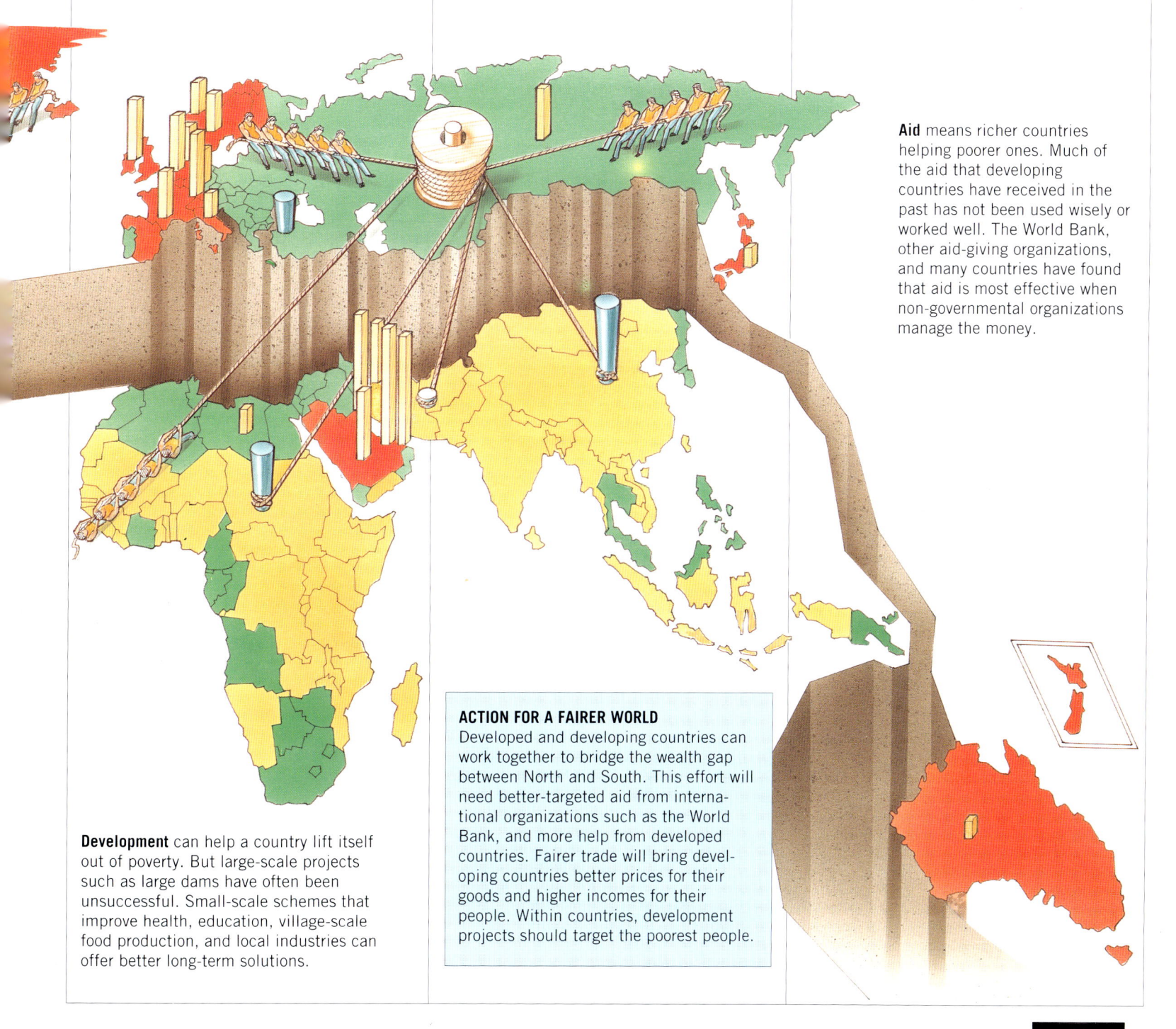

Aid means richer countries helping poorer ones. Much of the aid that developing countries have received in the past has not been used wisely or worked well. The World Bank, other aid-giving organizations, and many countries have found that aid is most effective when non-governmental organizations manage the money.

Development can help a country lift itself out of poverty. But large-scale projects such as large dams have often been unsuccessful. Small-scale schemes that improve health, education, village-scale food production, and local industries can offer better long-term solutions.

ACTION FOR A FAIRER WORLD
Developed and developing countries can work together to bridge the wealth gap between North and South. This effort will need better-targeted aid from international organizations such as the World Bank, and more help from developed countries. Fairer trade will bring developing countries better prices for their goods and higher incomes for their people. Within countries, development projects should target the poorest people.

43

USEFUL CONTACTS

UK GOVERNMENT BODIES
Countryside Commission, John Dower House, Crescent Place, Cheltenham GL50 3RA; tel 012242-521381, fax 01242-584270.
Department of the Environment, 2 Marsham Street, London SW1P 3EB; tel 0171-276 3000, fax 0171-276 0818.
Department of Transport, 2 Marsham Street, London SW1P 3EB; tel 0171-276 3000, fax 0171-276 0818.
English Nature, Northminster House, Northminster, Peterborough, Cambs. PE1 1UA; tel 01733-340345, fax 01733-68834.
Environment Agency, Waterside Drive, Aztec West, Almondsbury, Bristol BS12 4UD; tel 0117-962 4400; fax 0117-962 4409.
Forestry Commission, 231 Corstorphine Road, Edinburgh EH12 7AT; tel 0131-334 0303, fax 0131-334 3047.
Health and Safety Executive, Rose Court, 2 Southwark Bridge, London SE1 9HS; tel 0171-717 6000, fax 0171-717 6717.
Ministry of Agriculture, Fisheries and Food, Whitehall Place, London, SW1A 2HH; tel 0171-270 3000, fax 0171-270 8125.
Northern Ireland Office Department of the Environment, Clarence Court, Adelaide Street, Belfast BT2 8GB; tel 01232-540540.
Overseas Development Administration, 94 Victoria Street, London SW1E 5JL; tel 0171-917 7000, fax 0171-917 0019.
Scottish Office, Dover House, Whitehall, London SW1A 2AZ; tel 0171-270 3000, fax 0171-270 6730;
and also at
St Andrew's House, Regent Road, Edinburgh EH1 3DG; tel 0131-556 8400.
Welsh Office Environment Division, Cathays Park, Cardiff CF1 3NQ; tel 01222-825111, fax 01222-823204.

INDUSTRY BODIES
British Gas, Rivermill House, 152 Grosvenor Road, London SW1V 3JL; tel 0171-821 1444.
British Waterways, Willow Grange, Church Road, Watford, Herts. WD1 3QA; tel 01923-226422, fax 01923-226081.
Electricity Association Services, 30 Millbank, London SW1P 4RD; tel 0171-344 7244, fax 0171-931 0356; the trade association of the privatized electricity companies.
National Farmers' Union, 22 Long Acre, London WC2E 9LY; tel 0171-331 7200, fax 0171-331 7382.
Nuclear Electric, Barnett Way, Barnwood, Gloucester GL4 7RS; tel 01452-652855, fax 01452-652750.
Scottish Nuclear, Peel Park, East Kilbride G74 5PR; tel 013552-62626, fax 013552-62000.
Water Services Association and Water Companies Association, 1 Queen Anne's Gate, London SW1H 9BT; tel 0171-957 4567/0171-222 0644.

OTHER ORGANIZATIONS AND CAMPAIGNS
Many of the following supply free information and literature.
Action Aid, Hamlyn House, Macdonald Road, London N19 5LP; tel 0171-281 4104, fax 0171-263 7599.
Action for Southern Africa, 28 Penton Street, London N1 9SA; tel 0171-833 3133, fax 0171-837 3001.
Amnesty International, 99–119 Rosebery Avenue, London EC1R 4RE; tel 0171-814 6200, fax 0171-833 1510.
Anti-Slavery International, Unit 4, The Stable Yard, Broomgrove Road, London SW9 9TL; tel 0171-924 9555, tel 0171-738 4110.
Association for the Conservation of Energy, Westgate House, 2A Prebend Street, London N1 8PT; tel 0171-359 8000, fax 0171-359 0863.
British Red Cross Society, 9 Grosvenor Crescent, London SW1X 7EE; tel 0171-235 5454, fax 0171-235 245 6315.
British Trust for Conservation Volunteers, 36 St Mary's Street, Wallingford, Oxon. OX10 OEU; tel 01491-839766, fax 01491-839646.
British Wind Energy Association, 42 Kingsway, London WC2B 6EX; tel 0171-404 3433, fax 0171-404 3432.
Campaign against the Arms Trade, 11 Goodwin Street, London N4 3HQ; tel 0171-281 0297, fax 0171-281 4369.
Campaign for Nuclear Disarmament, 162 Holloway Road, London N7 8DQ; tel 0171-700 2393, fax 0171-700 2357.
Catholic Fund for Overseas Development, 2 Romero Close, Stockwell Road, London SW9 9TY; tel 0171-733 7900, fax 0171-274 9630.
Catholic Institute for International Relations, Unit 3, Canonbury Yard, London N1 7BJ; tel 0171-354 0833, fax 0171-359 0017.
Centre for Alternative Technology, Llangwern Quarry, Machynlleth, Powys SY20 9A2; tel 01654-702400, fax 01654-702782.
Charter 88, Exmouth House, 3–11 Pine Street, London EC1R OJH; tel 0171-833 1988, fax 0171-833 5895.
Children and War Project, Peace Pledge Union, 41b Brecknock Road, London N7 OBT; tel 0171-424 9444, fax 0171-482 6390.
Christian Aid, 35 Lower Marsh Street, London SE1 7RG; tel 0171-620 4444, fax 0171-620 0719.
Civic Trust, 17 Carlton House Terrace, London SW1Y 5AW; tel 0171-930 0914, fax 0171-321 0180.
Common Ground, 45 Shelton Street, London WC2H 9HJ; tel 0171-379 3109, fax 0171-836 5741.
Commonwealth Institute, Kensington High Street, London W8 6NQ; tel 0171-603 4535.
Community Service Volunteers, 237 Pentonville Road, London N1 9NJ; tel 0171-278 6601, fax 0171-278 1020.
Compassion in World Farming, Charles House, Petersfield, Hants. GU32 3EH; tel 01730-260791.
Concord Video and Film Council, 201 Felixtowe Road, Ipswich IP3 9BJ; tel 01473-715754, fax 01473-274531.
Conservation Foundation, 1 Kensington Gore. London SW7 2AT; tel 0171-823 8842.
Council for Education in World Citizenship, Weddel House, 13–14 West Smithfield, London EC1A 9HY; tel 0171-329 1711, fax 0171-329 1712.
Council for the Protection of Rural England, Warwick House, 25 Buckingham Palace Road, London SW1W OPP; tel 0171-976 6433, fax 0171-976 6373.
Development Education Association, 29–31 Cowper Street, London EC2A 4AP; tel 0171-490 8108, fax 0171-490 8123.
Earthwatch, Belsyre Court, 57 Woodstock Road, Oxford OX2 6HJ; tel 01865-311600.
Ecology Building Society, 18 Station Road, Cross Hills, Nr Keighley, West Yorks. BD20 7EH; tel 01535-635933.
Environmental Investigation Agency, 2 Pear Tree Court, London EC1R ODS; tel 0171-490 7040, fax 0171-490 0436.
Environmental Law Foundation, 42 Kingsway, London WC2B 6EX; tel 0171-404 1030, fax 0171-404 1032.
Environmental Transport Association, The Old Post House, Heath Road, Weybridge KT13 8RS; tel 0193-282 8882, fax 0193-282 9015.
Evergreen Trust, 50 Wilton Street, Old Basford, Nottingham, Notts. NG6 OER.
Fairtrade Foundation, 7th Floor, Regent House, 89 Kingsway, London WC2B 6RH; tel 0171-405 5942, fax 0171-405 5943.
Food Commission, 5/11 Worship Street, London EC2A 2BH; tel 0171-628 7774, fax 0171-628 0817.
Friends of the Earth, 26–28 Underwood Street, London N1 7JQ; tel 0171-490 1555, fax 0171-490 0881.
Friends of the Earth Northern Ireland, 56 Bradbury Place, Belfast 7; tel 01232-311555.
Friends of the Earth Scotland, Bonnington Mill,

USEFUL CONTACTS

72 Newhaven Road, Edinburgh EH6 5QG; tel 0131-554 9977, fax 0131-554 8656.
Greenpeace, Canonbury Villas, London N1 2PN; tel 0171-354 5100, fax 0171-696 0012.
HelpAge International, St James Walk, London EC1B 0BE; tel 0171-253 0253, fax 0171-895 1407.
Human Rights Watch, 33 Islington High Street, London N1 9LH; tel 0171-713 1995, fax 0171-713 1800.
Hunger Project Trust, Livingston House, Carteret Street, London SW1H 9DH; tel 0171-976 0332, fax 0171-976 0075.
Inland Waterways Association, 114 Regent's Park Road, London NW1 8UQ; tel 0171-586 2556.
Intermediate Technology, Myson House, Railway Terrace, Rugby CV21 3BR; tel 01788-560631, fax 01788-540270.
International Voluntary Service, Old Hall, East Bergholt, nr Colchester CO7 6TQ; tel 01206-298215, fax 01206-299043.
Latin America Bureau, 1 Amwell Street, London EC1R 1UL; tel 0171-278 2829, fax 0171-278 0165.
LETSlink, 61 Woodcock Road, Warminster, Wilts. BA12 9DH; tel 01985-217871.
Liberty (National Council for Civil Liberties), 21 Tabard Street, London SE1 4LA; tel 0171-403 3888, fax 0171-407 5354.
London Cycling Campaign, 3 Stamford Street, London SE1 9NT; 0171-928 7220.
London Development Education Centre, Instrument House, 207–215 King's Cross Road, London WC1X 8DB; tel 0171-713 7907.
Marine Conservation Society, 9 Gloucester Road, Ross-on-Wye HR9 5BU; tel 01989-566017, fax 01989-567815.
Medecins sans Frontiers, PO Box 138, Northampton NN3 6WB.
Medical Action for Global Security, 601 Holloway Road, London N19 4DJ; tel 0171-272 2020, fax 0171-281 5717.
Minewatch, 218 Liverpool Road, London N1 1LE; tel 0171-609 1852, fax 0171-700 6189.
Minority Rights Group, 379 Brixton Road, London SW9 7DE; tel 0171-978 9498, fax 0171-738 6265.
National Centre for Organic Gardening, Henry Doubleday Research Association, Ryton-on-Dunsmore, Coventry CV8 3LG; tel 01203-303517, fax 01203-639229.
National Peace Council, 88 Islington High Street, London N1 8EG; tel 0171-354 5200, fax 0171-354 5200.
One World Week, PO Box 100, London SE1 7RT; tel 0171-620 4444, fax 0171-620 0719.
Oxfam (UK and Ireland), 274 Banbury Road, Oxford OX2 7DZ; tel 01865-313600, fax 01865-312580.
Panos Institute, 9 White Lion Street, London N1 9PD; tel 0171-278 1111, fax 0171-278 0345.
Peace Child International Centre, The White House, Buntingford SG9 9AH.
Peace Education Project, Peace Pledge Union, 41b Brecknock Road, London N7 0BT; tel 0171-424 9444, fax 0171-482 6390.
Pedestrians' Association, 126 Aldersgate Street, London EC1A 4JQ; tel 0171-490 0750.
Permaculture Association, PO Box 1, Buckfastleigh, Devon TQ11 0LH; tel 01892-825049.
Pesticides Trust, 49 Effra Road, London SW2 1BZ; tel 0171-274 8895.
Plantlife, Natural History Museum, Cromwell Road, London SW7 5BD; tel 0171-938 9111, fax 0171-938 9112.
Population Concern, 231 Tottenham Court Road, London W1P 9AE; tel 0171-631 1546, fax 0171-436 2143.
Quaker Peace and Service, Friends House, Euston Road, London NW1 2BJ; tel 0171-387 6922, fax 0171-388 1977.
Refugee Council, 3–9 Bondway, London SW8 1SJ; tel 0171-582 6922, fax 0171-582 9929.
Royal Society for the Protection of Birds/Young Ornithologists' Club, The Lodge, Sandy, Beds. SG19 2GL; tel 01767-680551.
SAFE Alliance (Sustainable Agriculture, Food, and Environment), 38 Ebury Street, London SW1W 0LU; tel 0171-823 5660, fax 0171-823 5673.
Saferworld, 3rd Floor, 34 Alfred Place, London WC1E 7DP; tel 0171-580 8886; fax 0171-631 1444.
Save the Children, Mary Datchelor House, 17 Grove Lane, London SE5 8RD; tel 0171-703 5400, fax 0171-703 2278.
Scientists for Global Responsibility, Unit 3, Down House, Business Village, Broomhill Road, London SW18 4JQ; tel 0181-871 5175, fax 0181-877 1940.
Scottish Campaign for Nuclear Disarmament, 15 Barrland Street, Glasgow G41 1QH; tel 0141-423 1222.
Scottish Council for Civil Liberties, 146 Holland Street, Glasgow G2 4NG; tel 0141-332 5960, fax 0141-332 5309.
Soil Association/British Organic Farmers and Growers, 86 Colston Street, Bristol BS1 5BB; tel 0117-929 0661.
SOS Sahel, 43 Redcliffe Road, London SW10 9NJ.
Survival International, 11–15 Emerald Street, London WC1N 3QL; tel 0171-242 1441, fax 0171-242 1771.
Third World First, 217 Cowley Road, Oxford OX4 1XG; tel. 01865-245678, fax 01865-200179.
Tools for Self-Reliance, Ringwood Road, Netley Marsh, Southampton SO4 2GY; tel. 01703-869697, fax 01703-868544.
Tourism Concern, 65 Parkside, London SW19 5NN; tel. 0181-944 0464.
Traidcraft, Kingsway, Gateshead, Tyne and Wear NE11 0NE; tel. 0191-491 0591.
Transport 2000, Walkden House, 10 Melton Street, London NW1 2EJ; tel. 0171-388 8386.
United Nations Association, 3 Whitehall Court, London SW1A 2EL; tel. 0171-930 2931, fax 0171-930 5893.
United Nations Association of Northern Ireland, 1 Glesnharragh Gardens, Belfast BT6 9PE.
United Nations Children's Fund (UNICEF) UK, 55 Lincoln's Inn Fields, London WC2A 3NB; tel. 0171-405 5592, fax 0171-405 2332.
Voluntary Service Overseas, 317 Putney Bridge Road, London SW15 2PG; tel. 0181-780 2266, fax 0181-780 1326.
War on Want, Fenner Brockway House, 37–39 Great Guildford Street, London SE1 0ES; tel. 0171-620 1111, fax 0171-261 9291.
Waste Watch, Gresham House, 24 Holborn Viaduct, London EC1A 2BN; tel. 0171-248 1818, fax 0171-248 1404.
Water Aid, 1 Queen Anne's Gate, London SW1H 9BT; tel. 0171-233 4800.
Whale and Dolphin Conservation Society, Alexander House, James Street West, Bath BA1 2BT; tel. 01225-334511.
Wildlife Watch, The Wildlife Trust (Royal Society for Nature Conservation), The Green, Witham Park, Waterside South, Lincoln LN5 7JR; tel. 01522-544400, fax 01522-511616.
Willing Workers on Organic Farms, 19 Bradford Road, Lewes, Sussex BN7 1RB; tel. 01273-476286.
Women's Environmental Network, Aberdeen Studios, 22 Highbury Grove, London N5 2BR; tel. 0171-354 8823, fax 0171-354 0464.
Women's International League for Peace and Freedom, 7A Hepburn Road, Bristol BS2; tel. 0117-942 7878.
Woodland Trust, Autumn Park, Dysart Road, Grantham, Lincs. NG31 6LL; tel. 01476-74297.
World Development Movement, 25 Beehive Place, London SW9 7QR; tel. 0171-737 6215, fax 0171-274 8232.
World Disarmament Campaign, 45–47 Blythe Street, London E2 6LX; tel. 0171-729 2523.
World Rainforest Movement, 8 Chapel Row, Chadlington, Oxfordshire OX7 3NA; fax 01608-676743.
World Wide Fund for Nature, Panda House, Weyside Park, Godalming, Surrey GU7 1XR; tel. 01483-426444, fax 01483-426409.

GLOSSARY

Abortion The termination of a pregnancy before birth.
Agenda 21 The international programme of action for sustainable development agreed at the 1992 Earth Summit.
Aid Money grants and other kinds of assistance given by developed countries to developing ones.
AIDS Acquired immuno-deficiency syndrome, a condition in which the body loses its ability to defend itself against infections.
Apartheid The official South African government policy of racial segregation followed from 1948 to about 1990.
Arms trade The large-scale buying and selling of weapons and other military equipment.

Biotechnology Modern techniques using the chemistry of life to make food, drugs, or other products.
Birth control Limiting the number of children born, usually with contraception.
Birth rate The number of births each year per member of the population, or per 1000 people.
Blue-collar work Connected with manual industrial work.

Cancer A harmful tumour or growth that may spread from one part of the body to others.
Civilian A non-military person, a non-fighter in a war.
Civilization A developed and complex human society.
Civil war A war between different groups of people within the same country.
Cold War The semi-warlike relationship between the US-led West and the Soviet Union's Eastern bloc between 1945 and the late 1980s.
Commercial Connected with buying and selling goods or services.
Communicate To pass on information or another form of message.

Communist Connected with the belief (communism) in a classless society in which the means of production are owned collectively rather than privately.
Community A group of organisms living in one area and interacting with each other. Applied to human beings, the term suggests shared values or common experience.
Complementary medicine Traditional, alternative, and especially Eastern medical treatments used together with "Western-style" medical practices.
Consumption The act of using up a resource or product.
Continent A large landmass.
Contraception Using artificial or natural methods to prevent a new life forming in the womb.
Co-operative A form of organization in which people share ownership, management decisions, and income collectively.
Corporation A large business company.
Country A separate territory that rules itself independently.
Culture The ideas, beliefs, technology, and lifestyles of a particular society or group of people.
Cuneiform An ancient form of writing using wedge-shaped characters.

Debt Something owed, especially money.
Debt crisis The problems of developing countries since the 1980s in paying back the money lent to them by banks in developed countries.
Democracy Government by the people or their representatives with freedom of choice.
Developed country A country where large-scale industry, based on the burning of fossil fuels, is well established and usually the main source of jobs and wealth creation.
Developing country A country where farming, rather than large-scale industry, is still the main way of life.
Development Growth or progress; in economics, change whereby a community or a country becomes more effective at meeting its needs.
Distance learning Home-based study, at a distance from the school or college.

Earth Summit The United Nations Conference on Environment and Development (UNCED), held in Rio de Janeiro, Brazil, in June 1992.
Economy The activities involved in producing and consuming goods and services, and in managing resources and money.
Environment The surroundings in which a plant or animal lives.
Ethnic minority A group of culturally similar people seen as in some way separate from the majority population.
Export To sell to another country.

Fair trade A scheme to help low-income producers by buying their goods or services directly from them, rather than through agents, and at better-than-usual prices.
Family planning The use of birth control to limit the number of children born in a family and to ensure healthy gaps between births.
Forestry The management of forest lands.
Fossil fuels Coal, natural gas, and oil, created over millions of years by the decay of plant and animal remains.
Fuelwood Firewood.

Grass roots Describing ordinary people, as opposed to politicians and business and other community leaders.

Human rights Rights that every human being is entitled to as a member of society.
Hunting and gathering A way of life based on hunting animals and gathering wild food plants.

Illiterate Unable to read or write.
Immunize To protect a person medically against a disease.
Import To buy from another country.
Indigenous people People who have lived in a place, and close to the land, from the earliest times.
Industrial Revolution The 18th- and 19th-century development of large-scale industrial manufacturing in the countries of Western Europe and North America.
Industry Organized activity concerned with processing raw materials to produce things that people use, including food.
Infant mortality The number of young children who die in a given period of time.
Infection An invasion of the body by harmful microbes.
Informal economy Casual and at times illegal work, sometimes called black economy.
Information technology (IT) The use of computers to produce, store and communicate information.
Inner city Poorer parts of a city close to the centre.
Intermediate technology Cheap and simple technology suitable for use by poor people in developing countries.

Landmine An explosive device placed in the ground that explodes when stepped on or driven over.
LETS Local Exchange Trading Systems, a way of organizing work in a community based on a local "paper" currency rather than cash.
Life expectancy The average age of death of people in one area.
Literacy The ability to read and write.

Malnutrition A poor level of nutrition resulting from a lack of food or a poor diet.
Manufacturing Making products, especially factory goods, from raw materials.

GLOSSARY

Microchip A tiny semiconductor made out of silicon and carrying electronic circuits.
Migration Movement of people, animals, or plants from one place to settle in another.
Mineral Any solid, non-plant and non-animal, naturally occurring material.
Mortality rate The number of deaths per 1000 people per year.
Multinational corporation A large business company active in several countries; also known as a transnational corporation.

NGO Non-governmental organization.
Nomad A person who travels from place to place with domesticated animals to find pasture for them.
Non-governmental organization (NGO) An independent organization concerned with environmental issues, human rights, or similar problems.
North The developed countries of Western Europe, North America, Japan, and Australasia.
Nuclear winter Possible conditions after a global war using nuclear weapons.
Nutrition Nourishment with food.

Oral rehydration therapy (ORT) The taking of a simple salt-sugar-water solution by mouth to help recovery from severe diarrhoea.

Percent(age) Out of every 100.
Pollution Any substance that interferes with and harms natural processes when added to the natural environment.
Population A group of plants or animals of the same species in a certain area.
Primary health care Basic health care, advice, and treatment.

Radioactive The quality of giving out atomic radiation.
Raw material A naturally occurring substance used to make something else.
Recycling Using or processing materials (or energy) more than once.
Reforestation The replanting of trees and forests.
Refugee A person who flees from one country to another to escape danger or a severe problem.
Renewable Able to be used without reducing stocks of natural resources or causing pollution.
Resource A natural material or process (such as water flow) that provides energy or materials for people to use.
Rural Connected with the countryside.

Sanitation Equipment and facilities used to protect public health, especially with regard to toilets and water supplies.
Service industries Industries that provide services, such as transport and banking, not goods.
Shanty town A town or part of a town or city where poor people live in cheaply built houses or shacks.
South The developing countries of Africa, Asia, the Caribbean, Central and South America, and the Pacific.
Suburb An area, usually residential, on the edge of a town or city.
Sustainable development Development by which present generations of people meet their needs without reducing the ability of future generations to meet future needs.

Underdevelopment The condition of a developing country that is not using its resources mainly for its own benefit and where people have a low material standard of living.
Underemployed Lacking enough work or the kind of work for which a person is qualified.
Urban Connected with towns and cities.

West, Western Refers usually to North America and Western Europe but may include Australasia, Latin America, and other countries.
White-collar Connected with non-manual work.

47

INDEX

Headwords refer to information in texts and captions but not maps.
Bold page numbers refer to main entries in text.

abortions 21
Africa
  industry and wealth creation 29
  Zulu community 4
Agenda 21 23
aid 34, 42, 43
  comparison of donors 42
AIDS (acquired immuno-deficiency syndrome) 12
alcoholism 13
alternative medicine 20
Amnesty International 17
apartheid 17
architecture 26
arms trade 29, 36
art 26, 27
asthma 13

bananas 38
banks and loans to developing countries 35
"barefoot doctors" 21
biotechnology 28
birth control 12, 13, 20
birth defects 13
birth rates 12, 20
blue-collar jobs 8
Brazil
  cattle ranching 18
  improving the lives of city-dwellers 41
  industrialization 28
  Macuxi people 18
  working population 9
breastfeeding 21
Britain, manufacturing and trade 28
Buenos Aires, Argentina, homeless 40
Bushmen 6

cancer 13, 21
cattle ranching in Brazil 18
cave paintings 30
China
  birth control 20
  needs and rights 7
  nuclear weapons 37
  working population 9
cities **26–27**, **32–33**, **40–41**
  improvements **40–41**
  population growth 32, 33
  problems **32–33**
  renewal 41
civil wars 36
civilian deaths in wars 36
co-operatives 23
coal 28
Cold War 36
communications **30–31**
communities 22, 23, 38
community groups 22, 23, 38
community health care 21
computers 30, 31
consumer goods co-operatives 22, 23
cost of arms 36
Costa Rica, needs and rights 7
craft workers 14, 15
Cuba, healthcare 6

deaths
  of infants 7
  in wars 36
debt, and developing countries 35
Denmark, needs and rights 7
developed countries 7, 12, 13, 14, 15, 41
  civil liberties (basic freedoms) 6
  life expectancy 6
developing countries 7, 12, 13, 14, 15, 29, 40
  civil liberties (basic freedoms) 6
  debt 35
  life expectancy 6
  wealth 34
Dhaka, Bangladesh 26
diarrhoea, deaths from 13
diet, human 21
disease 21
  role of communications in prevention of 30
distance-learning 23
drug addiction 13
drugs in developing countries 13

Earth Summit 35
education 10, 11, 22
employment 8, 9, 14, 15, 29
energy efficiency 41
ethnic minorities and jobs 15

fair trade 22
family planning 20, 21, 30
farming 8, 14, 15
financial centres 26
fishing 9, 14, 15
food
  imports 12
  number of people lacking enough 7
France, nuclear weapons 37

General Motors, USA 28
Germany
  industrialization 28
  working population 8
global companies 28

health **12–13**, 30
health care **20–21**
heart disease 13
high-tech medicine 12
Homo sapiens 10
Hong Kong, shanty town 33
housing 7
human rights **6–7**, **16–17**, 19
  ways to help 17
Hungary, working population 8
hygiene 13

immunization 21
India
  community groups 38
  working population 9
indigenous peoples 17
industrial countries 29
industrial products 28
Industrial Revolution 28
industrialization, price of 29
industry **28–29**
infant death 13
informal economy 15
information technology 28, 30
inner cities 41
Intermediate Technology (organization) 22
Israel, nuclear weapons 37

Japan, manufacturing 29
Jerusalem 27

Kharochan, India, community group 38

landmines 37
language 30
law 27
LETS (Local Exchange Trading Schemes) 22
life expectancy 7
Lima, Peru, homeless 40
literacy 7, 10, 11
Local Exchange Trading Systems (LETS) 22
London 26
  Docklands 41

Mali, working population 9
malnutrition 13
manufacturing 28
Mecca 27
Mexico City 26
Middle Ages 26
Middle East
  industrialization 29
migrants 15
migration from the countryside 15
mineral 29
minorities 17
Minority Rights Group 17
money 26, 34
multinational companies 28

NGOs (non-governmental organizations) 22, 43
Nigeria, Benin City 27
non-governmental organizations (NGOs) 22, 43
North-South co-operation 42
North-South divide 34
nuclear weapons 37
nuclear winter 37

oil 29
oppression 16, 17
oral rehydration therapy (ORT) 13
Oxfam 23, 38

Paris 26
Peru, Q'Collor-Riti festival 24
pollution 18
population
  density 12
  increase 13
  world 12, 13
poverty 10, 16, 34, 42, 43
primary health care 20
printing 31
profits, in developed countries 34

radio 23, 30, 31
radioactive poisoning 37
Recife, Brazil 41
recycling 14, 41
refugees 16, 17
remote sensing 31
research and development 28, 29
Roman Empire 26
Rome 27
Russia, nuclear weapons 37
Rwanda, refugees 16

San people 6
satellite communications 30, 31
satellites 22
schooling 7, 10
self-help groups 20
Shanghai 26
shanty towns 32, 33, 40
  improvements to 40
slaves 16
small-scale manufacturing 28
smoking 21
speech 30
stress 13
Survival International 17

television 23, 30, 31
trade 34, 42, 43
traditional medicine 21
transport 41

UK, nuclear weapons 37
unemployment 14, 15
United Nations Children's Fund (UNICEF) 37
Universal Declaration of Human Rights 6, 16
urban life 32, 33
USA
  homeless and malnourished population 6
  manufacturing and trade 28, 29
  nuclear weapons 37
  working population 8

war **36–37**
  casualties 36
water, unsuitability for drinking 13
wealth
  creation, comparisons of 42
  gap 29, 34
weapons 29
  cost of 36
welfare 7
white-collar jobs 8
women
  and discrimination in the jobs market 15
  rights in developing countries 16
  in unpaid work 15
  in the workforce 8, 9
work 7
  lack of **14–15**
working population, global 8, 9
World Bank 43

Yugoslavia (former)
  war 36
  refugees 16